Presentations Plus

Presentations Plus

David Peoples' Proven Techniques

David A. Peoples

Atlanta, Georgia

John Wiley & Sons

New York · Chichester · Brisbane · Toronto · Singapore

Library of Congress Cataloging in Publication Data
Peoples, David A., 1930–
   Presentations plus.
   Bibliography: p.
      1. Business communication.   2. Public speaking.
3. Business report writing.   I. Title.
HF5718.P44   1988   658.4'5   87-21691
ISBN 0-471-63391-7
ISBN 0-471-63103-5 (pbk.)

Printed in the United States of America
10 9 8 7

Dedicated to my father and mother

Floyd G.
and
Teressa Z.

PREFACE

This is a book on how to develop and deliver an effective and exciting presentation.

It comes from success on the battlefield of business. It is based on years of doing, not on theory. Its methods are simple, practical, and proven. Its approach is effective when presenting to clients, customers, and prospects. It works equally well when used by managers or trainees.

The techniques of *Presentations Plus* have proven successful in the executive suite, the conference room, and the classroom. They are equally effective with an audience of one or an audience of hundreds.

The overall thrust of this book is to help you achieve your objectives and get results. It describes the Blueprint for Success—a step-by-step roadmap of what to do, and how to do it.

Dozens of real-life examples are included to illustrate each step.

If you are presenting to clients, customers, or prospects, this book will show you how to get more business with less effort by doing the right things the first time.

If you are presenting within your organization, this book will show you how to become too valuable to keep in your present job at your present pay.

If you want results, this book will show you how to persuade other people to a course of action you would like them to take.

In every company and organization there is a critical shortage of good presenters. If you learn to do well what most do so poorly, your success will be faster and farther.

So come along with me. Let's walk this road together. And I believe, you will walk the road to glory.

DAVID A. PEOPLES

Atlanta, Georgia
October 1987

A C K N O W L E D G M E N T S

Special thanks and appreciation to

Dr. Ed Metcalf
IBM
Atlanta, Georgia

Other reviewers and contributors

Mark Lloyd
President
Southern Business Communications
Norcross, Georgia

Joel Weldon
President
Joel H. Weldon & Associates
Scottsdale, Arizona

Tom Woods
President
Liveware Solutions International
Metairie, Louisiana

Thanks to Vivian for the typing, retyping, and retyping

And most of all

Thanks to "The Little Filly"
for help and encouragement

CLIP ART COURTESY OF

3M Company
Heading for Chapters 1,5,8,10,13,16

Artmaster Book Company
Heading for Chapters 2,3,11,15,17,18

Graphic Products Corp.
Heading for Chapters 4,7,14

Dover Publications
Heading for Chapters 6,9,12

C O N T E N T S

CHAPTER 1

What's In It For Me?

What's in it for you? Money, fame, and glory.

How would you like to:

Get more business with less effort by doing the right things the first time?

Become too valuable to keep in your present job at your present pay?

Have a sense of self-satisfaction, pride, and well-being from a job well-done?

Earn the respect, admiration, and envy of your peers?

Travel to meetings and conventions at resort locations?

Enjoy your work more than you ever have, and be happier than you've ever been?

"I'll take it—any of the above would suit me just fine."

WELL, how about *all* of the above?

The horse to ride to make it happen is to become a good presenter. I didn't say excellent or outstanding—I said just good. Because the rest of the world is so bad. You will do well if you just do good what most do poorly. In the valley of poor presenters, you can be the king of the mountain.

LET'S BE SPECIFIC

In your business, practice, or profession, how many prospects do you have to chase to get one new contract? One new customer? Or one new client?

Answer: lots of them!

Let's say, for example, that on average you have to chase four to get one. What if for every four you chased, you could get two instead of one? That would be a 100 percent increase in business over the old way . . . and would be accomplished in less time.

Now that's what I call getting more business with less effort!

I suggest to you that a way to make that happen is to give a formal presentation of your product or your services.

In the eyes of the prospect, this immediately makes you a breed apart. Your competition will follow the course of least resistance, which is phone talk, mail talk, desk talk, or at most, yellow-pad-and-pencil talk. You will have separated yourself from the pack and created an atmosphere of competence and professionalism if you ask for an appointment to make a formal presentation.

QUESTION:

Within a prospect's organization, how many people have to say yes before you get the order or the commitment? Almost always, more than one. Sometimes, four or more. That being the case, if you are really doing your job, you need to call on four or more people. That takes time. Now, folks, the only thing we have is time—and we all have the same amount. The biggest difference between us is how we use it.

I suggest that a formal presentation can be the catalyst for getting all the decision-makers together for a group presentation. The alternative is for you to make individual calls on each of them. So, instead of making four presentations—we make one presentation.

In addition to the obvious savings in time, there is another way a formal presentation shortens the decision-making process. If you call on the people individually, it often happens that a few days later one of them will call you up and say, "I've been thinking about our conversation and I have some more questions. Can you come back out?" There we go again—burning up our time. When you give a group presentation to all the decision-makers, the synergism of the group will tend to get all the pertinent questions on the table. All in attendance will hear the answers to each others' questions. So when it's over, it's over—there are no more questions.

There is another subtle but mighty important benefit that comes from making a formal presentation. The psychology of the situation creates an air of professionalism, which tends to eliminate (or at least minimize) discussions of concessions or special contracts.

Speaking of psychology, here is another piece of that same pie. If you request, prepare, and give a formal presentation, it tends to make the selection of the vendor or firm a big deal. And the bigger the deal, the more likely they are to pick the professional—and that's *you*.

The bigger the prospect, the more likely they are to expect professionalism. My experience has been that when you don't get the business you are rarely, if ever, told the real reason or the complete reason you lost. The easy out is to tell you that it was price. But often the real reason is that you did a sloppy, disorganized, disjointed, and unprofessional job of telling your story. In the prospect's mind, the quality of your presentation is a mirror image of the quality of your company, your product, your service, and your people.

There is another reason that has to do with your future. Let me put it this way. My company has the reputation of being a premier marketing organization. Yet in my company there is a critical shortage of good presenters. In fact, in most of our branch offices, there are few if any good presenters. Reason? The good ones have all been promoted. In fact, the shortage is so critical that we had to start promoting people who are not good presenters. So if you want a horse to ride to get ahead, here is a specific, identifiable way to make it happen.

Finally, strange things happen to those who do the work to become a good presenter. The quality that reflects in their presentations starts rubbing off in other areas. And next thing you know, everything they do has a higher level of quality. What started out as an improvement in one area became an improvement in all areas. Once you have tasted success in one area, you will settle for nothing less in other areas.

So let's get this show on the road. Remember the rule of 72? If you don't start within 72 hours, you'll never start. To start, turn the page.

CHAPTER 2

Putting a presentation together is like building a house. First we need a blueprint that shows us the components, their relationship to each other, and the priorities of things to be done.

DEFINE OBJECTIVES

The first priority in our blueprint is to define the objectives of the presentation. It is not only the first thing to be done—it is also the most important. Everything else we do—the content, the level of detail, the duration, and so forth—will stem from the statement of the objectives.

The objectives answer the question, "Why are we doing the presentation?"

When it's all over, what is it that you want the audience:

- To remember?
- To understand?
- To believe?
- Or what action do you want them to take?

"Well," you say, "it's self-evident." *Not true.* I challenge you to take out a pencil and write a very specific and precise statement of the objective of your presentation and get it right the first time.

Let's take an example.

Suppose the subject of the presentation is a computer software package that we sell.

You might then say that the objective of the software presentation is to explain the input, the processing, and the output reports of the package.

Or how about this? "The objective of this presentation is to give the audience an appreciation for the power, the ease-of-use, and the flexibility of this software package."

Now see what you think of this one? (I'm choosing my words carefully.)

"Ladies and gentlemen, the objective of this seminar is to give you *all* the information you need to make a *final* decision on this software package for your business."

Now that's what I call a well-thought-out and precise statement of objectives, that is, "To give you not one-half or three-quarters, but *all* the information you need to make (what kind of a decision?) a FINAL decision."

The last thing we want at the end of the presentation is an Alfred Hitchcock-type ending. We want the audience to clearly understand what we expect of them when it's all over. Just the fact that they understand our expectations increases the probability that it will happen.

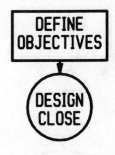

DESIGN THE CLOSE

I know it sounds backward to design the close first. You would think we would start with the opening. But look at it this way. From the presenter's point of view, the most important part of the presentation is the close. This is the acid test. At the close we either did, or didn't. They will, or they won't. They are sold, or they aren't.

The close is where we either accomplish our objective, or we don't. The close is the bull's eye. So, if we focus on the bull's eye first, then back up to the opening and the body, we will find that our entire presentation is more likely to focus on

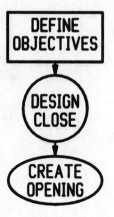

our objectives. What we say and what we present throughout the presentation will be designed to reinforce and enhance the close. We will end up with a well-structured and organized presentation that has singleness of purpose.

Remember when we were kids and we focused the sun through a magnifying glass onto a piece of paper until it caught fire? Here we are focusing the entire content of our presentation on the close. Let's not forget that the objectives, as embodied in the close, are the reasons for the meeting.

CREATE THE OPENING

The opening is the second most important part of the presentation.

What we need to recognize at this point, having designed the close, is that we have the opportunity for the opening to be a set-up for the close. The opening sets up the bowling pins which the close is going to strike.

For example, suppose in the opening we itemize the characteristics of an ideal

Lawnmower

Financial consultant

Computer software package

or whatever the product or service we're selling. Then in the close, we will summarize our product's/service's strengths.

Our strengths will, of course, turn out to be the same as the characteristics of the ideal product.

OUTLINE BODY

In the process of designing the body of the presentation, we need to break down the major subjects into their component parts. We need a detailed outline.

There are many approaches to the design of the outline and the body. For example:

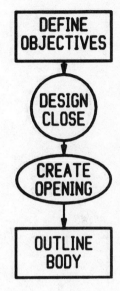

- Chronological
- Topical
- Categorical
- Problem/Solution
- Comparison/Contrast
- Ideal versus Reality
- Feature/Benefits
- Old way/New way
- Advantages/Disadvantages
- Goal/Roadmap
- Objections/Answers

For best results, use more than one of the above. For example, you might take a topical approach and show the old way versus new way and then the feature/benefits of the new way.

Now, using either a yellow pad or 3 × 5 cards, we follow the outline and write one key point per yellow pad page or for each 3 × 5 card. We write the key point using shorthand English with the focus on key words or phrases.

For example, a key point might be, "Explain true interest rate versus quoted interested rate."

Each page or card will be a candidate for a visual aid. Please note that I didn't say, "*Will* become a visual aid," just a *candidate* for a visual aid. More about that a little later.

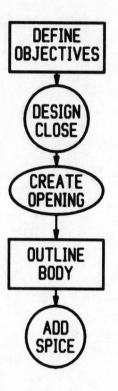

Now the fun begins. We lay out our pages or 3 × 5 cards on the living room floor in the sequence in which they will be presented. An excellent alternative is to tape them to a blank (just take the pictures down) wall in your office or at home. Please use masking tape, not Scotch tape. This is your storyboard.

Now we want to start talking through and thinking through the presentation from beginning to end. Several things will happen. First, you will notice that it will flow better if you change the sequence of some of the pages or cards. It will also become obvious that additional pages are needed for some areas while for other areas there is redundancy, or too much detail for the objectives of the presentation.

As you go through this process, have the objectives clearly displayed so that each page or card is evaluated relative to its contribution to the objective. There is just one test. If it doesn't contribute to the objectives, *don't use it.*

ADD SPICE

At this point, we have a well-structured, logical presentation. There's just one problem. It's dry, dull, and boring. It's all meat and potatoes with no sweets and no spices.

Our next mission is to breathe life, fun, and human interest into the presentation by adding spice. What are the spices? They are war stories, examples, analogies, gimmicks, jokes, and preplanned questions. Be sure they are related to the subject, and use them to illustrate or punctuate a point. You need a touch of spice every six to eight minutes.

So let your mind wander. Reach back into your past for stories, examples, experiences—anything you know of or have heard of that can add spice to your presentation. The difference between a ho-hum talk and an exciting presentation is the spice. So think up, dream up, or make up some spice. Believe me, people will remember the spice. And if you relate the spice to a key point, people will remember the key point. If you don't, they won't, because people forget 75 percent or more of what they hear within 24 hours or less.

DESIGN VISUAL AIDS

Back now to those sheets or cards lying on the living room floor or stuck on the wall.

Let's go through them again with this question in mind for the key point on each page: "Would a visual aid help to explain, understand, or punctuate this thought?" If the answer is "Yes," then you need a visual aid for that page. If the answer is "No," then you don't. If yes, what picture, symbol, or graphic would do the job best. There is just one rule—keep it simple.

Sketch in very rough form the design of the visual aid in the bottom right hand corner of the page or card. Do this with a soft pencil, not a pen. After a good night's sleep you will come up with better symbols for some of the pages.

TAILOR TO AUDIENCE

In very large measure, a key to the success of your presentation will be the perception by the

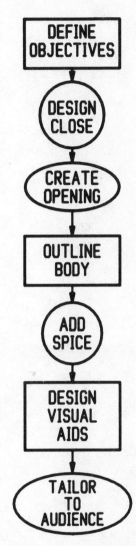

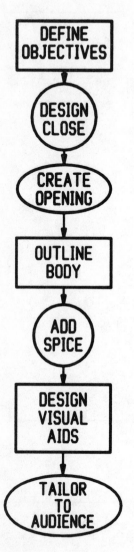

audience that this presentation was designed specially for them.

It is of critical importance that we have some understanding of the audience. A presentation on investment strategies to a group of rising business executives will have a different focus than investment strategies presented to an audience of retired people. We would like to know:

- Is the audience young or old? They have different objectives.
- Is the audience technical or general? They want different levels of detail.
- Are they blue collar, white collar, administrative, engineers, or sales? They have different interests.
- Do they have some knowledge or no knowledge of the subject? You may bore them or mystify them.

It should not be the responsibility of the audience to sort through a general purpose presentation to find those parts that apply to them. It is your responsibility to tailor the presentation to the audience.

Usually you have a pretty good idea of the different type groups you will be presenting to. What we want to do is decide in advance what changes need to be made to tailor the presentation to the different groups, then create the changes at the same time we are creating the presentation.

Often it's not as big a job as you might think. Sometimes a modification of the opening, a change in the close, the use of a different example, or skipping over some of the detail will do the trick.

CREATE CHEAT SHEETS

Here we go again. Back to those sheets on the living room floor or stuck on the wall. We have decided some of them will have a visual aid to support and enhance the presentation, and some will not. In either case, we decide once and for all what the first three to five words will be when we come to this page or this visual.

So the first thing on our cheat sheet are the first three to five words we will use to introduce each key point. Next we will have key words or phrases for the details on this key point.

The final item on this cheat sheet is special instructions to ourselves. For example, if we plan to ask a question, we would have the question written out. If we wanted to pass out a handout, then we would have a note to remind us to pass out a handout. Or, if we were going to draw a graph on blank flip-chart paper, we would have a miniature of that graph on our cheat sheet.

In other words, the cheat sheets are a shorthand script of the entire presentation. *Nothing is left to chance.* Everything that happens is planned in advance, with key words and phrases noted on the cheat sheets.

REHEARSE, REHEARSE, REHEARSE

Do not play it by ear. Everybody who is good at anything got that way by working, doing, practicing, and rehearsing. There are no short cuts.

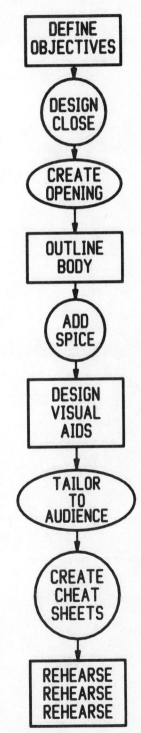

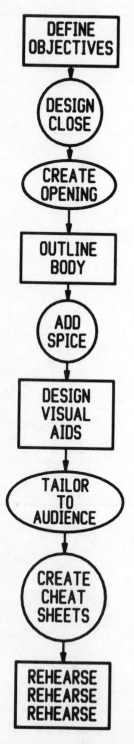

So let's just make up our minds to do what we know we have to do.

SUMMARY

We can summarize the Blueprint for Success by asking ourselves the following questions:

1. What is my objective?
2. How will I close the presentation?
3. How will I open the presentation?
4. How will I organize the body?
5. How will I get their attention?
6. How will I keep their interest?
7. What questions will I ask?
8. What questions will they ask?
9. What visual aids will I use?
10. How will I tailor the presentation to the audience?
11. What notes do I need?
12. How many times should I rehearse?

WHAT ABOUT THE CANNED PITCH?

What we have just described will get the job done the way it should be done for presentations you develop.

But what about those presentations developed by someone else, and handed to you or mailed from Headquarters. Some come complete with a detailed script. If you present it as is, it's guaranteed to come across as stiff, formal, and mechanical. To be successful, a presentation must be a human experience. That means it has to be a reflection of your chemistry and your personality—not that of a remote script writer who has never met you.

Just as it was important to tailor the presentation to the audience, it is also important to tailor the presentation to the presenter. The good news is that 95 percent of the work has already been done. With just a little effort we can have a whiz-bang presentation that looks like you and sounds like you.

Guess where we start? You got it. We start on the living room floor. Lay it out and start talking through and thinking through the presentation the way you would give it.

One of the characteristics of these types of presentations is that they tend to have too many visuals in too much detail. So have your hatchet handy, and get ready to cut.

Next we add spice. *Our spice.* Presentations from Headquarters and most other canned presentations are notorious for their absence of spice. No wonder so many presentations are so boring. So add life by adding spice.

Then we tailor the presentation to *our* audience, and create *our* own cheat sheets. If the presentation comes with a script, it's easy. Just sort through the script, and look for key words and phrases that make sense to you. If some are missing, make up your own.

When you finish with the presentation, you may have to send it back. If you might be giving it again sometime, keep your cheat sheets. They are a roadmap to easily recreate the presentation the way you gave it.

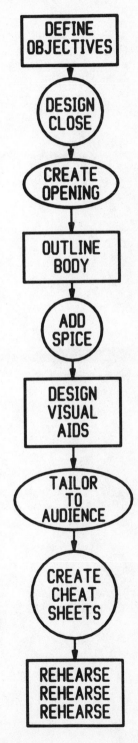

CHAPTER 3

Design The Close First

From the presenter's point of view, the most important part of the presentation is the close. It is at the close where you either accomplish your objective, or you don't. Do they believe? Do they agree? Will they commit? Will they act? Will they order? The answers to these questions tell you how well you accomplished your objective. The objective is a statement at the beginning—the audience gives you their answer at the end.

You have only one chance at a professional close. So important is the close, that we plan it and design it from the very beginning. We want the objective and the close to dictate the contents of the entire presentation. This will keep our eye on the target.

Let's look at it from the audience's point of view. It is at the close where they hear what they came to hear. Everything up to now has been in support of the close. We have been making our case, providing the evidence, and proving our points. Now we are ready to deliver the package, gift wrapped, with a red bow.

They will remember best what they hear last. So when it's all over and the people are leaving, what is it that you want them to have in their heads?

This technique is the same as that used by some writers of mystery novels. They conceive the ending first, then work backward to develop the rest of the story.

You might think the close is obvious and easy. I suggest to you that this is not the case. The secret is to leave the audience wishing for more, while at the same time feeling good because they got more than they expected.

You must write out the last two or three minutes of the presentation, and then do what the pros do—memorize it. That's right, memorize it. (What are you doing that is more important than giving this audience the very best you've got to give?) If you had just three minutes to tell someone the bottom line of your entire presentation, what would you say? That requires some planning and heavy thinking. Your entire presentation is no better than the close. So do it right. Take a tip from Broadway—the best song is the last song. Have them leaving singing your song.

The worst possible close is one that just peters out and sinks into the sunset with the comment, "Well, that's about all I have, folks. Are there any questions?"

What about questions at the end? The problem is, this is the high point of your entire presentation—this is the climax. If you now enter into a prolonged Q-&-A period, you will detract from your close, bore most of the audience, and quickly lose the enthusiasm of the group. Moreover, it's completely unnecessary. If you plan the questions as part of the presentation, there will be no questions at the close. They will all have been answered.

An entire chapter on questions and answers is coming up. For now, let's remember that the time to not only answer questions, but also ask questions, is *during* the presentation, not at the end of the presentation.

If, in spite of this sermon, you still feel the need to say, "Are there any questions?" do it just before the close—not after.

Before we get to specific examples of a close, let's talk about that mind-changing drug—HUMOR.

Humor is one of the world's greatest medicines. It is also one of the most powerful weapons of the presenter. It directly attacks hu-

```
I FULLY REALIZE THAT I HAVE
NOT SUCCEEDED IN ANSWERING ALL
OF YOUR QUESTIONS...INDEED,
I FEEL I HAVE NOT ANSWERED ANY
OF THEM COMPLETELY.  THE ANSWERS
I HAVE FOUND ONLY SERVE TO RAISE
A WHOLE NEW SET OF QUESTIONS, WHICH
ONLY LEAD TO MORE PROBLEMS, SOME
OF WHICH WE WEREN'T EVEN AWARE WERE
PROBLEMS.


TO SUM IT ALL UP...IN SOME WAYS
I FEEL WE ARE AS CONFUSED AS EVER,
BUT I BELIEVE WE ARE CONFUSED ON
A HIGHER LEVEL, AND ABOUT MORE
IMPORTANT THINGS.
```

FIGURE 3A Humor is a mind changing drug. It breaks down resistance and the tendency to say *No.*

man resistance and breaks down the mental barriers. It can annihilate the natural tendency of the human defense mechanism to say *No.*

Humor can be particularly effective as a warm-up to the close—especially if it's dry wit and poking fun at yourself.

Figure 3A is an example of a warm-up to a close.

THE HAPPY ENDING CLOSE

Now, let's talk in concept about the design of a close.

Here is an example of an approach that we might call the Happy Ending Close.

Let's suppose that we are selling or promoting a product or service that we will call "X." We structure the presentation so that in the opening we present:

- The *characteristics* of an ideal "X" or
- The criteria for selecting the best "X" or
- The functions of a comprehensive "X."

In the body, we talk about the *functions, features, benefits, and advantages* of our "X."

Then in the close we summarize the *strengths* of our "X."

Guess what? Our strengths turn out to be exactly the same as:

- The characteristics of an ideal "X" or
- The criteria for selecting the best "X" or
- The functions of a comprehensive "X."

The key to the Happy Ending Close is to design the close first. Having done that, you back up to the opening and structure it to be exactly compatible with what you now know the close will be. Or simply put, the close provides the perfect answers to the questions raised in the opening. The only way you can make that happen is to design the close first. If you don't, you may raise questions in the

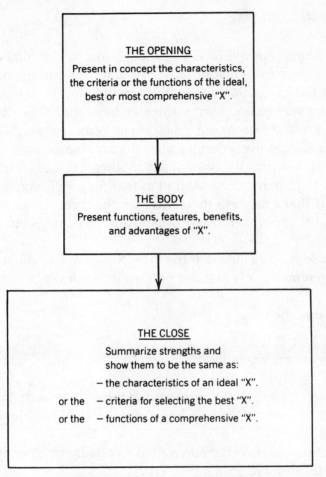

FIGURE 3B The Happy Ending Close

opening for which you have weak answers, or no answers in the close.

If you use this approach properly then you can ask for and get the audience's agreement on key points in the opening. If they agree with the opening, then the close becomes a "gotcha."

THE FUNNEL CLOSE

Here's another approach. Let's suppose you have a total of 15 key points in your presentation. The day after the presentation, how many of the key points do you think people will remember? That's right. Not very many. Maybe three or four. And they may not be the three or four we would prefer them to remember. After all, he who emphasizes everything, emphasizes nothing.

Suppose we approach the subject another way. Let's start with the day after and make the assumption that they will remember three things. If that's the case then what are the three things we would like them to remember? These will be the three things our close will focus on.

Suppose we conclude that the three things we would like the audience to remember is that our product or service is:

1. Comprehensive
2. Easy to use
3. Easy to maintain

Now we can design the close around these three central thoughts. We classify each of the 15 key points within the three central thoughts.

Our close can now be represented pictorially by three funnels as shown in Figure 3C.

THE ICEBERG CLOSE

Having established the close, we can now back into the opening and the body to provide a logical structure and flow to the presentation.

What we have done is to categorize 15 independent key points into three summary conclusions that we want the audience to remember.

The point of this structure is that even though people will not remember the 15 supporting key ideas, they will remember that the proof of each of the three central thoughts was convincing, and at the time they heard it they were in agreement.

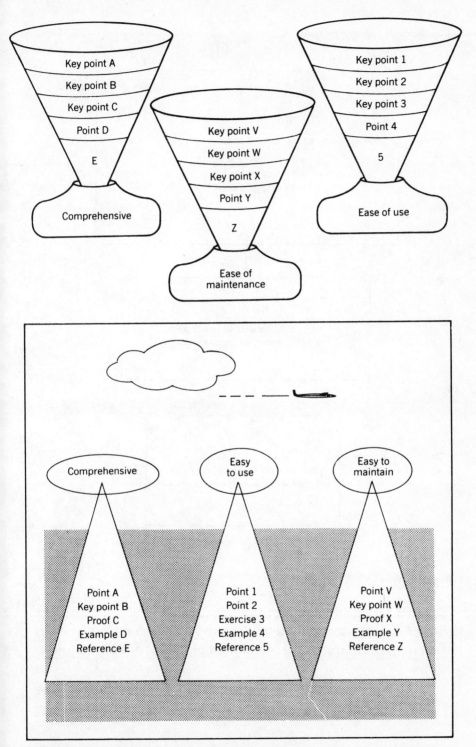

FIGURE 3C If we use the funnel close we can control what the audience will remember. A variation of the funnel close is the iceberg close.

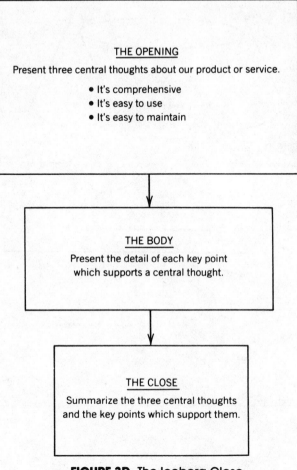

FIGURE 3D The Iceberg Close

So even though they forget the details, they will remember the three truths you want them to retain. And it doesn't matter whether the subject is a computer, an investment program, or a lawn mower.

THE SHOTGUN CLOSE

Well, you say, that sure makes a lot of sense. I like the structure, the flow, and the logic. However, the nature of my presentation doesn't lend itself to that structure. I have many key points to make and they aren't well related, so they don't fit into your funnels. In fact, they are almost the opposite of a funnel—they are more like a shotgun.

Suppose for example, you are in personnel or training. Your job is to give a company orientation presentation to new employees. You have 20 unrelated key points to present.

How in the world are you going to get them to remember 20 key points? Here's how you do it. We call it the Shotgun Close.

The secrets to success of the Shotgun Close are:

1. Repetition
2. Verbal participation
3. Written participation

We design the close to be in the form of a verbal test that we all take together. The test consists of multiple questions—one for each key point. Figure 3E is an example of a Shotgun Close.

Again, having now designed the close, we can back up to the opening and the body.

This approach is not only different, it is also stimulating, interesting, and is the best way for an audience to remember a large number of points.

You should think through each question carefully to make it interesting and provocative. Also, provide space on the handout for the audience to write down the correct answers.

This technique applies the principles of Confucius:

- *They hear it.*
- *They see it*—if you have proper visual aids.
- *They do it*—by the act of writing the correct answer.

<u>HOW GOOD IS YOUR INVESTMENT IQ?</u>

True or False

1. T F Out of every 100 people, 26% are flat broke at age 65.

2. T F 40% of all people living in poverty are women.

3. T F The cheapest way to borrow money is to use the method that will discount interest.

4. T F Baron de Rothchild said, "Common stocks are the 8th wonder of the world."

5. T F The technical method of forecasting future stock movement is correct only 75% of the time.

6. T F Persistent pattern in the stock market occur as frequently as 75% of the time.

7. T F The greater the risk - the lower the commissions a stockbroker gets.

8. T F 70% of all stockbrokers own mostly over-the-counter stocks - not Blue Chips.

9. T F 10% of all people who invest in the stock market over 10 years do not make money.

10. T F Of the Forbes 400 richest men and women in America, over one half made their fortune in the stock market.

11. T F Mark Twain said, "July is the most dangerous month to speculate in stocks."

12. T F Stocks recommended on <u>Wall Street Week</u> have typically out performed the market average by 5-10% within the next two months.

13. T F The five year performance of mutual funds has been significantly greater than the market average.

14. T F The size and scope of the large institutional investor gives them a significant advantage over the individual investor.

15. T F If you had followed Howard Ruff's advice over the last five years, you would have had an average annual return of 24%.

16. T F Professional investment advice has been wrong 25% of the time.

17. T F There are more millionaires per capita in Maine than any other state.

18. T F Solid investment advice for the last 20 years would have been to -- buy good stocks and hold on to them.

19. T F Over the last five years you would have done better in Old Master Paintings than anything else.

20. T F You can defer taxes - but never avoid them completely.

FIGURE 3E The Shotgun Close. Creative questions can get attention, keep interest, and provide a format for the presentation.

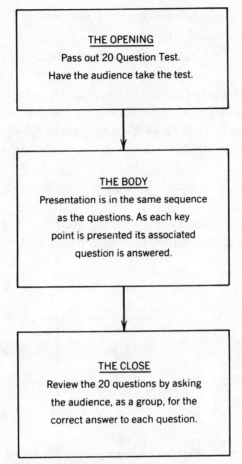

FIGURE 3F The Shotgun Close

Built into the structure of the presentation is

1. Repetition
   a. Seen at the beginning
   b. Elaborated on during the presentation
   c. Reviewed at the close

2. Participation
   a. Each individual takes the test during the opening.

b. The answers are written on the handout as they are covered in the presentation.

c. The group retakes the test verbally during the close.

They won't remember the 20 questions. But any time one of the 20 questions is asked, they will remember the answer.

By the way, the answer to all 20 questions is False.

THE "I'M HERE TO HELP" CLOSE

Here's another approach called the "I'm Here To Help" Close. Suppose we have a picture of the close that looks like Figure 3G.

CLIENT OBJECTIVES	HOW I CAN HELP	FEATURE OF MY PRODUCT OR SERVICE
Increase productivity	A._____	1._____
Reduce cost	B._____ C._____	2._____ 3._____
Improve service	D._____ E._____ F._____	4._____ 5._____ 6._____

FIGURE 3G "I'm Here to Help" Close

Now we can back up to the opening and body.

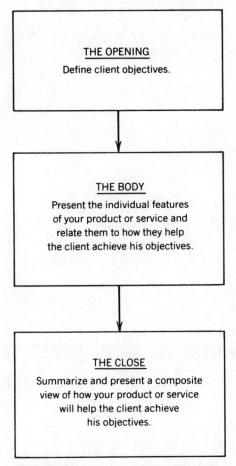

FIGURE 3H "I'm Here to Help" Close

THE JIGSAW PUZZLE CLOSE

Next we have a close called the Jigsaw Puzzle Close.

Here we have in our mind the image of a close that looks like Figure 3I.

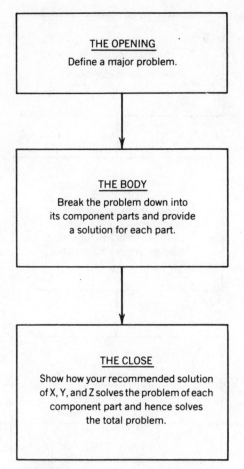

FIGURE 3I The Jigsaw Puzzle Close

The idea is that we define a major problem, then break the problem down into its component parts (the seven pieces of the puzzle). We then provide a solution (X, Y, or Z) for each component part of the problem.

The purpose of the close is to show that all component parts of the problem are solved by our recommendation of X, Y, and Z.

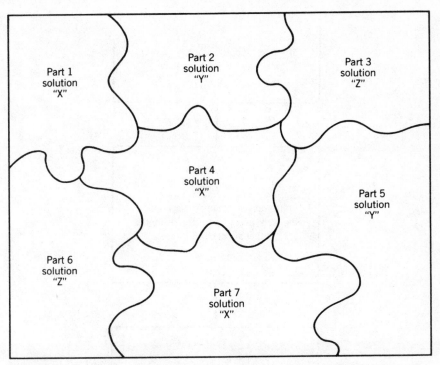

FIGURE 3J The Jigsaw Puzzle Close. Define a problem. Break it into parts. Show that all parts are solved by our recommendation of X, Y, and Z.

PREDICTIONS OF THE FUTURE CLOSE

Here is a popular close. You almost can't lose with this one. You simply predict what's going to happen in the future.

People like good news. If you are predicting the future, you can make the news as good as you want. And the farther out the prediction, the more plausible it may seem. Also, this type of close gives you an aura of wisdom and insight that is rare among mortal beings.

If our close is Predictions of the Future, then we can back up to the opening and the body.

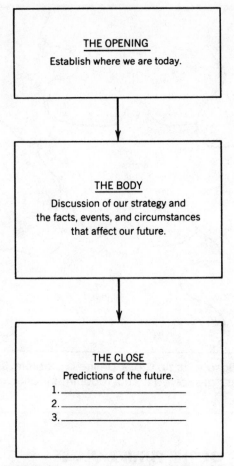

FIGURE 3K Predictions of the Future Close

THE BRIDGE OVER TROUBLED WATERS CLOSE

Another approach is the Bridge Over Troubled Waters Close.

The idea here is that we define a goal that the audience would like to achieve. The problem is that there are major obstacles to achieving this goal. These are shark-infested waters. There is danger, risk, and uncertainty in achieving our goal. The odds of the audience making it alive with their health intact are not good. Fortunately, your firm provides a bridge over these troubled waters that

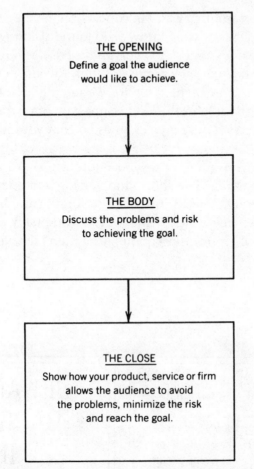

FIGURE 3L The Bridge Over Troubled Waters Close

will allow them to safely cross over to the other side and get the pot of gold at the end of the rainbow.

THE AUTHORITATIVE QUOTE CLOSE

Another idea for a close is to build it around some authoritative quotation which is in direct support of your objective.

For example, listen to this close.

"And now, in summary and in conclusion, let me tell you the John Ruskin story. Does anyone know who John Ruskin was? He's dead, you know. He died almost 100 years ago. He was a real ugly fellow, too. (Show a transparency picture of John Ruskin.) One of the ugliest fellows I've ever seen. Why are we talking about John Ruskin? We're talking about John Ruskin because you often quote something he wrote. There's hardly a week goes by that you don't quote John Ruskin.

"But when you quote him, you quote the shorthand version of something he wrote. The shorthand version you quote says, 'There ain't no free lunch.' But I want to show you the longhand version of 'There ain't no free lunch'—the way he originally wrote it (show transparency of John Ruskin quote), and then I'll have a footnote for you."

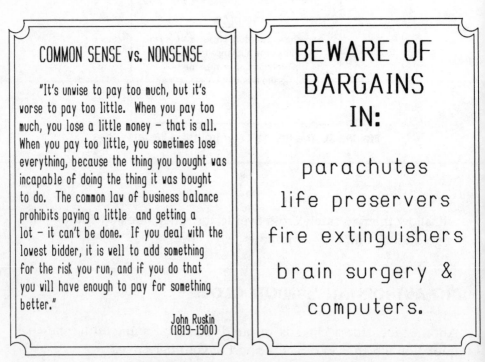

FIGURE 3M The Authoritative Quote Close

Footnote: "And so in conclusion I say to you: beware of (show Beware of Bargains transparency) bargains in

parachutes,
life preservers,
fire extinguishers,
brain surgery, and
computers."

The authoritative quote close was designed to appeal to logic, and common sense.

THE EMOTIONAL CLOSE

Some people are more inclined to an Emotional Close. For example:

"And so in summary and in closing I say to you: I love you, I want you, I need you, I can't get to where I want to go without you. And I believe in you. I believe the power within you and the support behind you are infinitely greater than the task before you.

"So come along with me. Let's walk this road together. And I believe (show transparency), I believe, I believe you will walk the road to Glory."

FIGURE 3N An Emotional Close

Other sources of a close are personal experiences of yourself or of someone with whom the audience would recognize or identify. These must relate and tie-in to your closing theme. They are most effective when they paint a picture of the following:

From failure to success

From depression to elation

From weakness to strength

From poor to rich

From sick to strong

From defeat to victory

From the bottom of the heap to the top of the mountain

You get the idea. And if the punch line can be told with an Alfred Hitchcock closing style—they'll never forget it.

If your presentation has to do with the selling of a product or service, don't forget to ask for the order. Trouble is, I have had people say to me, "I can't do that—I'm not a salesman." To which I say, "Would you feel comfortable saying, 'Mr. Smith, do you think we could do business together?'" They say, "Sure, I can say that." To which I reply, "Good, it's the same thing."

Figure 3O is an example of a three-step close that presents a plan or solution, asks for a decision or commitment, and gives the action to take or the document to sign.

These are just a few examples of closes. As you think about it you will come up with others—your imagination is your only limitation.

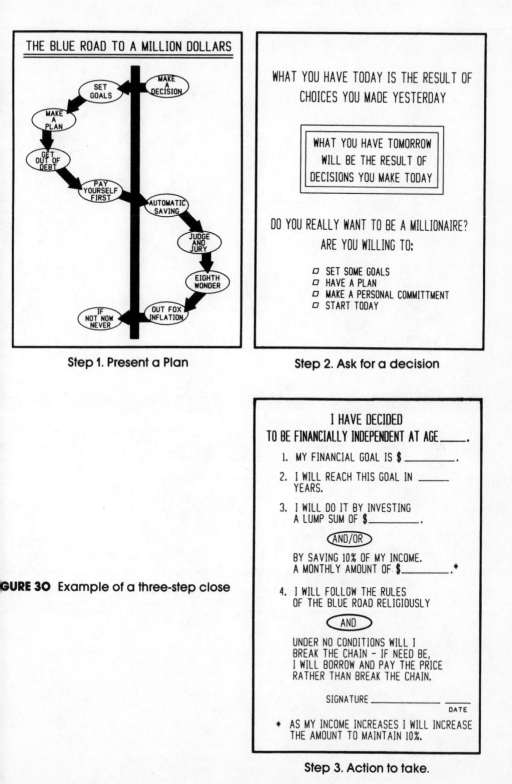

THE BLUE ROAD TO A MILLION DOLLARS

SET GOALS

MAKE A DECISION

MAKE A PLAN

GET OUT OF DEBT

PAY YOURSELF FIRST

AUTOMATIC SAVING

JUDGE AND JURY

EIGHTH WONDER

IF NOT NOW NEVER

OUT FOX INFLATION

Step 1. Present a Plan

WHAT YOU HAVE TODAY IS THE RESULT OF CHOICES YOU MADE YESTERDAY

WHAT YOU HAVE TOMORROW WILL BE THE RESULT OF DECISIONS YOU MAKE TODAY

DO YOU REALLY WANT TO BE A MILLIONAIRE? ARE YOU WILLING TO:

☐ SET SOME GOALS
☐ HAVE A PLAN
☐ MAKE A PERSONAL COMMITTMENT
☐ START TODAY

Step 2. Ask for a decision

FIGURE 30 Example of a three-step close

I HAVE DECIDED
TO BE FINANCIALLY INDEPENDENT AT AGE_____.

1. MY FINANCIAL GOAL IS $_____.

2. I WILL REACH THIS GOAL IN _____ YEARS.

3. I WILL DO IT BY INVESTING A LUMP SUM OF $_____.

AND/OR

BY SAVING 10% OF MY INCOME.
A MONTHLY AMOUNT OF $_____.*

4. I WILL FOLLOW THE RULES OF THE BLUE ROAD RELIGIOUSLY

AND

UNDER NO CONDITIONS WILL I BREAK THE CHAIN – IF NEED BE, I WILL BORROW AND PAY THE PRICE RATHER THAN BREAK THE CHAIN.

SIGNATURE _____ _____
DATE

* AS MY INCOME INCREASES I WILL INCREASE THE AMOUNT TO MAINTAIN 10%.

Step 3. Action to take.

You never get a second chance to make a first impression.

Just as we tend to judge a book by its cover, so your audience will come to an opinion of you in about three minutes.

Other than the close, the opening is the most important part of the presentation.

The first and most obvious thing people will notice is whether the meeting starts on time. What are you going to do? Here it is time to start and only half the people are present. So we should wait another 5 or 10 minutes, right? Wrong. The first rule is: The meeting starts on time, if you're in charge of the meeting. What's the big deal about waiting a few minutes? ("Everybody does it.")

Let's look at it this way. What do you think is going through the mind of the people who were there at 9:00 and the meeting finally starts at 9:20? Something like, "My time is as valuable as yours—if you were going to start the meeting at 9:20, why didn't you announce it for 9:20? The next time you schedule a meeting for 9:00 do you think I will be there at 9:00? Not on your life." In fact that's probably the very reason half the people weren't present at 9:00 for this meeting.

By the way, how long would you guess the 10-minute coffee break is going to last? And when you announce that the meeting will reconvene after lunch at around 1:00, when do you think you will really start? Well, you get the idea—we bring it on ourselves.

Or, has this ever happened to you? You have a 9:00 flight and a tight connection at the next stop. Some 200 people are strapped in their seats at 9:00. But it's not until 9:20 that the plane begins to taxi with the explanation that we were waiting on a few late arriving passengers. How did that make you feel?

The next order of business is your introduction. We'll look at it from two points of view. First, if someone is introducing you; second, if you are introducing yourself.

If your company is like mine, introductions tend to be very stereotyped. After awhile they all sound alike: full of acronyms, strange sounding titles, and job descriptions that most people never heard of and could care less about.

The only titles that really get people's attention are:

President of _____

Inventor of _____

The first man to _____

Discoverer of _____

Author of _____

Winner of _____

And so on.

If you have one of those handles, you've got it made. If you don't, let me suggest a change of pace. Something so radically different from most bios that it will catch the audience completely off guard, and give them a warm feeling about you before you even open your mouth.

The centerpiece is human interest. A natural human question is, "I wonder what he or she is really like?" So forget the wordy titles and meaningless job descriptions. Delve back into your past and put together a human interest bio. No one but you has been where you've been, done what you've done, and had your experiences. Let them hear the uniqueness that is yours alone. If you do it right, I promise you it will bring a smile to their faces and warmth to their hearts.

Be sure you include in your bio the experience and credentials that qualify you to speak on your subject.

Figure 4A is an example of a human interest bio.

If you are introducing yourself, the one thing you must convey to the audience is your credibility in the subject matter you are going to present. But we need to be careful because in the mind of the audience there is a fine line between establishing credibility and being boastful, cocky, or worst of all, arrogant.

Don't cross the line.

Here is how we handle it. Say just enough to lay the foundation of credibility. The additional details that might sound boastful we will build into the presentation at strategic points as references, or as examples to punctuate a key point. We just include them as key word notes on our cheat sheets.

DAVE PEOPLES

GREW UP IN THE SHADOW OF THE GREAT SMOKEY MOUNTAINS IN THE HILLS OF EAST TENNESSEE

IS TRAINED AND EXPERIENCED IN:

1. THRASHING WHEAT
2. KILLING HOGS
3. "BACKER SETTIN" (TOBACCO SETTING)
4. PACKSADDLE PICKIN
5. "MADER GROIN" (TOMATO GROWING)
6. POST HOLE DIGGING
7. RABBIT CLEANING
8. THE AUSTRIAN SCHOOL OF ECONOMICS
9. COMMODITIES FUTURE TRADING

HAS LIVED IN

1. VALLEY HOME, TENNESSEE
2. BIG SPRINGS, TEXAS
3. MORRISTOWN, TENNESSEE
4. CINCINNATI, OHIO
5. THE FOOTBALL STADIUM
6. CHANDLER, ARIZONA
7. CHATTANOOGA, TENNESSEE
8. KINSTON, NORTH CAROLINA
9. THE SIGMA CHI HOUSE
10. GREENVILLE, SOUTH CAROLINA
11. BARRE, VERMONT
12. BIG RAPIDS, MICHIGAN
13. OSAN, KOREA
14. ASHEVILLE, NORTH CAROLINA
15. ATLANTA, GEORGIA

HE HAS BEEN:

1. A HUNTER
2. A TRAPPER
3. A FISHERMAN
4. A FARMER
5. A LABORER
6. A STONECUTTER
7. A QUARTERBACK
8. A JET FIGHTER PILOT

AS AN IBM MARKETEER, HE HAS:

1. BEEN A DIRECTOR OF THE 100% CLUB
2. MADE 13 100% CLUBS
3. AND 3 GOLDEN CIRCLES

AND MAY BE THE ONLY MAN YOU WILL EVER MEET WHO OWNS A WATERFALL.

FIGURE 4A A human interest bio will get their attention, put a smile on their faces, and bring warmth to their hearts.

Depending on the type of meeting you are part of, you might want to go around the room and have each person introduce themselves and give a little personal information such as name, what they do, and where they come from.

I always disliked these introductions because it always seemed like the person just in front of me was a natural born comedian who was full of humor, wit, and clever remarks. I would follow him with a mundane name, rank, and serial number.

Here is an idea for getting around that problem if the audience comes from different organizations. It also has the effect of getting people to know each other and warms up the crowd. Have each person interview the person sitting beside them. You provide a format for the interview by passing out the interview form included here.

After a few minutes the teams reverse roles and the interviewee becomes the interviewer. Each person then introduces to the group the individual they interviewed by providing the answer to at least five of the questions on the interview form. It's a lot of fun, and really loosens up the audience.

It also provides you, the presenter, with some valuable information about the audience mixed in with the levity. This is information you need to do three things:

1. Level-set the audience.
2. Tailor the presentation.
3. Set the level of expectation.

LEVEL-SET THE AUDIENCE

What is this level-set the audience business? This refers to the different levels of knowledge and experience on the part of the audience about the subject. To the extent that you have a great variance you run the risk of boring some of the people and confusing others. What we should do is pick a base level for the start of the presentation. If we set this level higher than the knowledge level of some of the people, then we need to bring them up to the base level.

ANSWER ANY 5 OF THE FOLLOWING

1. COMPANY, DEPARTMENT OR CITY _____.
2. EVERY NEW YEAR'S EVE YOU RESOLVE _____.
3. YOU HAVE ALWAYS WANTED TO _____.
4. YOUR'RE A SUCKER FOR _____.
5. IN HIGH SCHOOL YOU WERE KNOWN AS _____.
6. YOUR VERY FIRST JOB WAS _____.
7. THE ONE THING YOU'VE LEARNED IS _____.
8. THE BEST PART OF YOUR JOB IS _____.
9. THE WORST PART OF YOUR JOB IS _____.
10. YOUR GREATEST ACHIEVEMENT WAS _____.
11. YOUR FAVORITE ACTOR/ACTRESS IS _____.
12. YOUR SPOUSE THINKS YOU'RE _____.
13. MOST PEOPLE DON'T KNOW THAT YOU _____.
14. IN ADDITION TO WORK, YOU'RE ALSO GOOD AT _____.
15. THE BEST MOVIE YOU EVER SAW WAS _____.
16. IF YOU COULD DO IT ALL OVER YOU WOULD _____.
17. THE BEST BOOK YOU EVER READ WAS _____.
18. YOUR FAVORITE FOOD IS _____.

FIGURE 4B Answer Any 5

We do this by identifying the key points of the premise, which become the base level, and reviewing these points briefly and in summary form. One effective technique for accomplishing this is to put these points in the form of questions that you address to the group. This will not only level-set the group, it will also let those who have little or no knowledge know in a dramatic way that the premise is well-known and accepted.

TAILOR THE PRESENTATION TO THE AUDIENCE

We tailor the presentation by learning as much as possible about our audience in advance of the meeting. In the introductions you will pick up additional information for the tailoring of the presentation to the audience. The introduction technique also affords you the opportunity to add real-time spice to both your opening and the close. Here's how. Have a pen or pencil handy during the introductions. As certain information comes to light during the introductions that you can relate and tie in to the content of the opening, make a note of it and the name of the individual linked to it. Then in your opening refer to that person by name and the subject of his or her comment.

For example, suppose Joe Smith says, ". . . and I'm here because I need help in so and so." Then in your opening you can say, "And Joe, I'm pleased to tell you that we are going to cover so and so in great detail. In fact, by the time we finish, you will. . . ."

Then at the close, guess what? That's right. We reference Joe and his comment again—perhaps with a direct question such as: "And in summary, Joe, have these key points helped you with so and so?" Well, of course he will say yes. And you've already got a testimonial.

That kind of personalization adds spice and breathes life and spontaneity into your presentation.

In the final analysis, our objective is to tailor the presentation to the interest of the group. The first opportunity we have to do that is in the opening. You will be amazed at the effect minor modifications will have on the initial audience perception—even though you're using an off the shelf or canned pitch.

Speaking of tailoring and effective openings, let me tell you one of the most clever things I have ever seen in my life.

I used to run a class for new managers in my company. Its purpose was to give them management exposure to the company and provide them with information on management philosophy, rules of the road, and Do's and Don'ts. To accomplish this we had guest presenters representing key functional areas of the business.

One of the key areas was personnel. To present this we had the manager of personnel. Well, this guy was an absolute master at tailoring a presentation to an audience. Let me explain.

If you think about it and put yourself in the place of a new manager, there are certain obvious subjects you want to know about and will have questions about in the area of personnel. Things like merit pay increases, appraisals, how to handle the poor performer, and so on.

This guy had given this presentation so many times that he knew there were always 8 to 10 subjects that new managers would like to discuss. And they were always the same 8 or 10 subjects. He had a prepared presentation on each of these subjects.

So in his opening, rather than introducing the subjects he was going to talk about, he would walk up to a blank flip-chart stand, and ask the audience what they would like to talk about in the area of personnel management. As subjects were volunteered from the floor he would write them on the flip chart. Guess what? They were always the same 8 or 10 subjects. The only difference was the sequence. He had the material for each subject in a manila folder. He just rearranged the sequence of the folders, and began presenting the subject on the flip chart.

I saw him do this many times. It never failed. He always presented the same subjects. He was always giving the same presentation he had planned to give, anyway—just in a different sequence.

The impact on the audience was dramatic. Not only was he talking about what they wanted to talk about, but they were dumbfounded at his in-depth knowledge and statistical quotes about what appeared to be spontaneously volunteered and unrehearsed subjects.

There is another type of tailoring we need to think about.

If you are one of multiple presenters on a program, you need to understand what came before you and what's coming after you. If you do, then you will be able to tie-in to material that has already been covered and reference things that are yet to come.

Again, you can create the perception that your presentation was specifically designed to fit right here, and to complement the other presentations.

There is nothing worse than finding out after the fact that 50 percent of your material was covered by the previous speaker, or, even worse, that you flat out contradicted the previous speaker and with no explanation.

So if you can, sit in on the other presentations—at least the one just preceding yours. If you can't do that, try to get a detailed briefing in advance from the host.

SET THE LEVEL OF EXPECTATIONS

Finally, with or without introductions, we need to set the expectation level of the audience. This needs to be communicated as part of the statement of objective of the presentation. The audience needs to know, when it's all over, what they will get out of it. We must avoid the kind of situation where the audience thinks the presentation is about saving on taxes while the thrust of your presentation is on financial planning and strategy. This is nothing more than the simple rule of tell them what you're going to tell them. We want no surprises at the end.

Sometimes the hardest part of anything is just getting started. So here's an idea for the start of the opening that's always a winner.

Say something nice about the audience, their company, their occupation, their organization—whatever the common denominator is that brings them together. And if you can, relate anything you can in your background to their common denominator. That makes you one of them.

Your most listened-to sentence is your first sentence, so it deserves a lot of thought. In fact, you can set the tone for the entire presentation with just one sentence. For example,

"I'm here to talk about how to get more business with less effort by doing the right things the first time."

or

"I want to talk about how you can become too valuable to keep in your present job at your present pay."

or

"I'm not here to talk about hardware, software, or applications. I'm here to talk about money, fame, and glory."

or

"Let me ask you a question. In this business, how many frogs do you have to kiss to find a prince?"

These all appeal to the interest of the group, and explain to them in one sentence why it's in their best interest to pay attention to what you have to say.

If you cannot articulate a reason for the audience to pay attention to what you have to say, then you have nothing to say to this audience. You are wasting their time and your time.

The best example I have ever heard of someone explaining to me why it was in my best interest to pay attention happened in Texas.

I was going through jet fighter pilot training. Before they strap the stove pipe on you, you have to go to ground school to learn the electrical system, the fuel system, and so on. One day the instructor walked into class and held up in his hand a red ribbon with a pin at the end. He said, "Gentlemen, do you know what this is?" Well, of course we didn't know what it was.

He explained that this was the safety pin from the ejection seat of an F-86 Saber Jet, and that for the next hour he was going to lecture to us on how to eject from an F-86 Saber Jet and survive. Then when we finished the lecture we were going out that door to the parade grounds where there was an actual ejection seat mounted on a vertical railroad track. And, one at a time we were each going to be strapped into that seat. We would pull down our visors, pull up the left arm rest, pull up the right arm rest, then pull the trigger underneath the right arm rest—and when we did, a live 20 millimeter cannon shell was going to explode under our you-know-what, and we were going to be shot straight up.

Do you think he had our attention? Let me tell you, every man in that room could have given that lecture. That instructor had explained very well a selfish reason for us to pay attention to what he had to say.

So early in the opening be sure you answer these kinds of questions.

Why are we here?

Why is it important?

What's in it for me?

How can I use it?

What will I get out of it?

People will pay attention and listen to what you have to say if they can see an advantage to themselves. The advantages can take many forms:

Material gain

Management approval

Prestige

Self-advancement

Imitation of others

Social approval

Self-satisfaction

Sense of accomplishment

Peace of mind

Satisfy curiosity

We won't belabor the *statement of objectives* except to remind ourselves of two things:

1. It's the most important part of the opening.
2. It must be structured to support and complement the close. A way to think about the relationship of the opening to the close is to think of the "before" and "after."

Now we come to the single most important thing you can do to ensure a successful opening and a good first impression. *Memorize the first two minutes.* To do that you will have to write out the words in advance—think about them, modify them, get them just right for you. Then when you stand up and start and the anxiety level is at its highest, you don't have to think up what you're going to say. Just turn the brain switch to on and out it comes.

The alternative is not very attractive. In fact, it's kind of scary. The alternative is trying to think up what you're going to say, and create a good first impression, while your sweaty palms are at their worst.

Simple solution—*memorize the first two minutes.*

Do not—repeat—*do not* take the first 10 or 20 minutes to cover administrative detail. Remember, other than the close, the opening is the most important part of the presentation. Don't blow it with a downer. Spread those administrative details out during the day or cover them after the opening, not before.

Speaking of Don'ts, if you hand out an agenda or show an agenda on a visual, just show the subject names. Do not show the start and stop time for each subject. If you do, the audience will be preoccupied with time, the schedule, and where you are in the program. If you get behind schedule, they will think you did a poor job of planning or you're not in control.

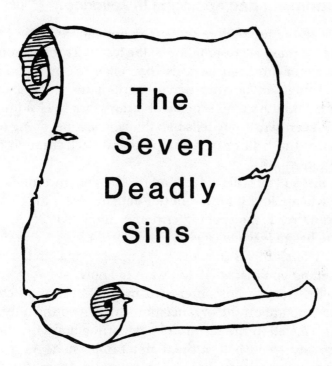

The
Seven
Deadly
Sins

Here are seven guaranteed ways to give a dull, dry, and boring presentation.

SIN #1 Show an Organization Chart, Tell the History of Your Department, and Apologize in Advance.

It happens all the time. Here comes the hot-shot flying in from the home office to make a presentation to the locals. Through some misguided sense of direction he feels compelled to show you, as the very first thing, an organizational chart of his department and where it fits into the grand scheme of things back at Headquarters.

Then his keen sensitivity tells him that you are just dying to know the details of the history of his department back through the last three reorganizations.

Finally, just so you will understand that he's not incompetent (just busy), he will apologize for the out-of-date material, the small print that you can't read, the spelling errors, running over time, and the fact that he has to leave to catch a plane.

The irony of all this is that he thinks he's giving a good presentation and telling you just what you want to know.

In fact, the people most interested in an organization chart are the people who are on the organization chart. And the only people who are interested in the history of a department are the people in the department—and half of them aren't interested. As for all the apologizing, I sometimes would like to say to them, "Instead of apologizing for the way it is, explain to me why you haven't corrected it." I betcha that would get it fixed real quick!

SIN #2 Do Not Explain Any Reason Why the Subject Has Any Value to the Audience.

If you cannot articulate a reason for the audience to pay attention to what you have to say, then you have nothing to say to the audience. And that's the problem. Many presentations are put together for a mass audience, with no tailoring and no spice, to present material that's of great interest to the presenter, but of little interest to the audience.

Here's the acid test. How many people do you think would show up if you charged them 10 bucks a head to get in to hear what you have to say?

SIN #3   Use a Presentation Designed for One Audience—for a Different Audience.

This is my all-time favorite sin. You can spot this sin in the first 60 seconds. These presenters usually start their presentations with— guess what?—an organization chart. Their purpose was to update Headquarters' management on the wonderful job their department is doing. That same presentation is then delivered to the troops in the field. Do you think they care?

Another example is the use of an internal presentation of a new product as a sales presentation to prospects. Do you think the position of a product within a product line has anything to do with why a prospect should buy it?

SIN #4   Tell the Audience More Than They Want to Know.

This sin is worse than just boring an audience—it is self-defeating. I would guess that over 90 percent of all presentations could be given in less time and more effectively. And often in *substantially* less time. I do a presentation on our corporate strategic direction that used to take me 2½ hours. I now do it in one hour and it's much more effective.

I have another presentation on financial planning that I can do in 3 hours, or 1½ hours. People seem to like the 1½-hour version as well or better than the 3-hour version.

Let's look at it this way. How many sermons, sales pitches, meetings, or conferences have you ever attended that were too short? How many times have you ever heard anybody say, "It was a wonderful presentation but it was too short." If CBS can tell us the world news in 30 minutes, just maybe you could tell your story in less time than you think.

SIN #5   Turn the Lights Out and Show Slides or Foils While Reading a Script.

How many presentations like this have you had to sit through? And what if it's right after lunch? And what about that script? Do you think the person reading it is the person who wrote it? (Or was it an English major from Berkeley?) And don't you feel sorry for them when they get out of sync and the words are one step ahead or behind the slides? And what about the close? When the lights come on, the audience en masse will blink their eyes, shake their heads, yawn, and stretch. What drama.

SIN #6   Read Verbatim Every Word on Every Visual.

If your entire presentation consists of nothing but reading verbatim every word on every visual, then the audience can with good reason say, "I don't have to come to your meeting. Just mail me a copy of the handout. I can read." 'Nuff said.

SIN #7   Do Not Rehearse—Play It by Ear.

If there ever was a guaranteed formula for failure, this is it.

If you want to stumble, fumble, and sing off key, this is a sure way to do it. If that doesn't bother you, think of the audience. They deserve something better than an amateur reading a script, or trying to think up what he is going to say on the audience's time.

What is it that makes you think you can get by with what the pros would never try: performance without practice?

There is no easy and painless road to a good presentation. As in every other endeavor, you have to pay your dues.

CHAPTER 6

FLIPS
FOILS
OR
SLIDES

What media should we use to help us tell our story?

Before we jump into the pros and cons of flip charts versus overheads versus slides, let's recognize that the presentation may have been shipped down to you as a package from Headquarters complete with a script. You might conclude that the work is all done. Not true. A word or two, and a lot more, about that at the end of this section. Let's now assume you are going to create your own presentation. What is the best media or visual aid to use?

Before we talk about what's best, let's talk about what's worst. The answer to what is worst is: nothing.

The audience's attention level, comprehension, and retention, as well as *your* persuasiveness, will be greatly enhanced if you will use visual aids.

LET'S TALK ABOUT FLIP CHARTS

Flip charts are the workhorses that have been around forever. A flip chart stand is standard equipment in most conference rooms and all hotel/motel meeting rooms.

They are effective for small groups.

They allow—in fact, demand—that the lights be full-up.

They are relatively easy to make.

They create an atmosphere of informality and promote audience participation.

They are easy to change, add to, and in general keep current.

They are economical.

On the Other Hand

They are not practical if group size is larger than 50 seated with tables in front of them, or around 80 seated theater-style.

They tend to get dog-eared and tattered with use and travel.

They are somewhat awkward to travel with.

OVERHEAD TRANSPARENCIES

(Sometimes referred to as foils or just overheads.)

Overheads are an all-purpose media that is probably used more than any other today—and for good reason.

They are suitable for audience sizes from very small up to 400. Yes, I said up to 400.

They are relatively easy to create, and look professional.

They are easy to maintain and travel well.

They lend themselves to creativity, color, overlays, drawings, cartoons, and so forth.

Overheads can and should be used with the lights reasonably bright (contrary to what you might think).

Overheads give the presenter complete control of the presentation (unlike slides).

They provide an informal atmosphere.

They promote audience participation.

They are not expensive if you have access to a personal computer with a quality printer and a desk-top foil-making machine. If you have neither but do have a copier, you can still get the job done. (More about that later.)

They are easy to maintain and keep current.

They are easy to replace as they age (fingerprints, lint, and yellowing).

On the Other Hand

They are not practical for group sizes in excess of 400.

With heavy use they collect fingerprints and lint. Over time they tend to turn yellow. The simple solution to all of this is to simply keep the originals and make new transparencies.

SLIDES

This is the big time. This is for the convention of 800 people. This is the businessperson's answer to Hollywood.

> The major advantage of slides is that for a large audience (over 400) it's the only medium they can clearly see.
>
> Slides look professional.

But everything else about them is a downer.

> They are formal.
>
> They usually require the lights to be down.
>
> They inhibit discussion and participation.
>
> They often come from the home office with a script that is terrible.
>
> They are expensive.
>
> They are difficult, awkward, and expensive to change and keep current.
>
> They are impersonal.
>
> The presenter loses flexibility and control over the presentation.

There is another aspect to slides if used for a small group that is difficult to put into words. Let me see if I can explain it this way.

One of the big events in my company is the annual kick-off meeting in January held at all branch offices throughout the country. For this occasion, material is sent to the branches from Headquarters about new products, new services, new marketing programs, and so on. But for the sales force, the biggest announcement of all is the Sales Compensation Plan or simply the Sales Plan, as it is called in the bull pen.

If a sales plan is announced with technicolor slides and a Headquarters script, it is received with skepticism, doubt, and the certainty that it must not be any good or else they would not have gone to so much trouble and expense to try to convince us how great-it-is-gonna-be. Get the picture?

VISUALS WITHOUT VISUALS

Saving the best for last, we now come to the presentation technique for small-to-medium-size groups that is the absolute best for ensuring:

Attention

Comprehension

Retention

Persuasiveness

and the overall effectiveness of the presentation.

The bad news is, it is also the most difficult.

Let me tell you a story.

One of the best marketing tools we ever had was not a sales pitch, but an educational seminar on computer concepts for seven days. Is that a misprint? No, I said seven days—and at a remote location. Well, I guess that's fine to train programmers. But wait, this is not for programmers. The only people allowed to attend are presidents and chairmen of the board.

There are no prepreparedvisual aids of any kind. The only props for seven days are two flip-chart stands with blank paper and magic markers. The presenter creates his visuals as he talks by writing and drawing on the flip charts in real-time. Although this gives the appearance of spontaneity, believe me, seven days of material has been carefully dissected, organized, and preplanned for each blank page. Exact words that will go on every page are preplanned, their position on the chart is preplanned, and the color is preplanned. Multicolors are used for emphasis. Heavy use is made of graphics and pictorial representations, and the drawing is carefully rehearsed. Nothing is left to chance, including *which* flip chart is used, *when* it is used, and *what* is left to viewing on *stand one* as the presenter moves to *stand number two*. Corners on strategic flip chart pages are turned down so the presenter can refer back to them at a future, predetermined time.

This requires a true professional who can write and talk at the same time, and has the timing and presence to control the audience. This style is more a controlled group discussion than it is a presentation. The blank flip charts, and writing or drawing in real time, not only give the presentation spontaneity but create an illusion for the audience that the presentation is being created just for them. In fact, at preplanned points in the presentation, the material is covered in such a way that an obvious question is not addressed. That question is always asked by someone in the audience. And the presenter—while giving the appearance of answering a question of interest to the audience—is merely continuing the preplanned sequence of the presentation.

To finish the story: This seminar always got outstanding critiques from top management. For the first time in their lives they truly understood computer technicians at their level. More importantly, from my company's point of view, the attendees could now envision an expanded role of the use of a computer in achieving their business objectives as the computer became their friend and a business tool, rather than a mysterious and expensive bookkeeping machine. "Well," you might say, "I'm sure as heck not up to presenting seven days' worth of material." But how about using this technique for 30 minutes? And if you're not up to that, how about for 30 seconds? More about that coming shortly.

BLACKBOARD

A variation of drawing your visual in real time on blank flip charts is to use a blackboard. Of course there aren't many black ones left. Mostly they are green, brown, or white. If it's a true chalkboard, it's messy. In fact, you can always spot the people using these. They are the ones who wash their hands *before* they go to the bathroom.

Also, the clarity of a chalkboard often leaves something to be desired. However, the new white boards that take felt-tipped (multicolored) magic markers are excellent. Many of these are set up as three, four, or more panels across the front of a room. They are excellent for presenting a progression or flow, such as the development and evolution of computer software over the years. It's helpful to be able to reference back and show similarities and contrasts. Comprehension is better if the audience can see the entire picture before them.

This is the technique, along with discussion and participation, that is used so effectively at the Harvard Business School.

It has two major disadvantages. To pull it off well, you have to be good at it. You have to be able to write and talk at the same time. That means lots of work and lots of rehearse.

The other disadvantage is that the presentation is not portable. You can't take the blackboards with you. In the world of business that problem automatically rules out many presentations.

DESK-TOP FLIP CHARTS

Here we are talking about $8\frac{1}{2} \times 11$ representations of flip charts— usually in a three-ring binder with a cover that is designed to make it pop up and sit up.

On the surface this would appear to be the ideal medium for a one-on-one presentation. But let's talk about that.

Certainly it is better than nothing. But remember, one of our objectives is to be a breed apart—to stand out from your competition. If your competition has anything, it is probably a desk-top flip chart.

Also, a desk-top flip chart comes across like a T.V. commercial. Many of them are designed as a self-contained sales pitch—you really don't have to say a word—and that's the problem. Because that's the way it comes across. The prospect could legitimately say, "You didn't have to make this trip. You could have just mailed me a copy of the flip charts." Of course, he won't say that. But what he will say is, "That's fine for other people, but we're different." Translated that says, "You just gave me a general purpose sales pitch, and I'm not a general purpose person, and we're not a general purpose company. I'm special, and we're special."

Do not underestimate the psychological impact of a one-on-one stand-up, flip chart, or overhead transparency presentation. For many of your prospects or clients, this will be the first time in their lives anyone has made such a presentation to them. The unspoken words in this scene say to the prospect, "You are a very important person. I sincerely want your business and I am willing to stand up and work for it."

Remember, one of your objectives is to get a 100 percent increase in your business. A stand-up presentation can make it happen. Now I know it seems a little silly and like a big waste to be making a formal presentation to one person. But my experience has been that of *all* the things I've ever tried, nothing—*nothing*—has been as effective as a one-on-few, stand-up presentation for getting results you can hold in your hand or take to the bank.

Just try it.

THE TALKING PICTURE BOX

A kissing cousin to the desk-top flip chart is the self-contained movie/picture/sound machine where the only thing the presenter has to do is to push the go button. Presenters and teachers love it because it requires no work on their part. Only problem is, clients won't like it for all the same reasons they don't like the desk-top flip chart, but more so.

But let's be fair. There is one excellent use of these gadgets, and that is to present complex concepts, ideas, or interrelationships. Sometimes you can accomplish in 10 minutes with pictures what is well near impossible with just words. But the machine is simply a piece of the total presentation and is used only to do those parts of the presentation it can do better than a presenter. The cardinal sin is relying on a machine as a total substitute for a human being. People don't want to do business with a machine—they want to do business with a human being.

A high-tech variation of the above is the ability to hook up a personal computer to a projection machine and project on a larger screen. The high-tech boys really like this because they can interact live with the computer and show the results on the screen.

But the lights have to be down, and even then the clarity is terrible. Worse still, the screen is often full of numbers and very confusing. What the presenter perceives as an excellent demonstration of ease-of-use and flexibility, is perceived by the audience as complex and hard to use.

MAGNETICS

The concept here is to attach magnetic spots to the back of lightweight pieces of cardboard. Then, in a predetermined sequence, you attach them to a blackboard that attracts magnetics.

Although little used, magnetics can be very effective in explaining complex subjects and relationships where the end result is built up piecemeal of its component parts.

This is a solution for those who can't talk and write on a blackboard at the same time.

Magnetics are probably best when used in conjunction with another medium.

THE REAL THING

Where the size, cost, and convenience of an item permit, always show the real thing. Pass it around the audience.

For some types of products you can even dissect them or have a cutaway so the audience can see and touch what they would normally never see. And while we're talking about it, how about giving one away as a door prize? That's called audience participation.

APPLES AND ORANGES

Objects can be used as symbols or as gimmicks to focus attention and emphasize key points.

For example, in comparing your product to competition, you could have an apple in one hand and an orange in the other as you talk about comparing apples to oranges.

Now, you might say that is really cornball. But let me tell you, people remember that stuff. And that says a lot, since most people remember very little.

WHAT'S BEST

Well, that's it, folks . . . now which of the above is the best visual aid of all to use?

I think the most correct answer is "none of the above."

I think the best visual aid to use is a combination of at least two. One can be used for the mainstream presentation, and the other for contrast, change of pace, and emphasis.

For example, a mainstream presentation that uses overhead transparencies can be combined with writing or drawing on a flip chart.

This technique breaks the monotony, forces you to walk, lends spontaneity and credibility, heightens audience attention, and improves retention.

So choose your weapons, and let's get this show on the road.

CHAPTER 7

Putting
The
Act
Together

Now it's time to take those sheets that were on the living room floor and create the finished product.

In the Blueprint for Success we had suggested that you rough out in the southeast corner of the cheat sheet the visual aid that would go with that key point. But we need to talk in more depth about the Why, When, and What of visual aids.

Of the total inventory of knowledge you have in your head, 75 percent came to you visually; 13 percent through hearing; and a sum total of 12 percent through smell, taste, and touch. In fact, if I show you a pictorial representation of a key point and say nothing, the comprehension and retention will be 3½ times greater than if I just say the words without a picture. And if I do both, that is, give you the words and the picture, the comprehension and retention will be six times greater than just saying the words.

Have you ever come back from a vacation and found out that you missed a meeting? Then when you asked somebody what happened at the meeting, they told you in three minutes what happened in an hour-long meeting. That's what I mean by retention.

Here is a trick I have pulled. Scares me to death every time I do it, but it's never failed yet. At conventions or conferences where I am the speaker on day #2, I remind the attendees that the first speaker, just 24 hours ago, talked for 32 minutes. I then say, "If you could remember just 25 percent of what the first speaker said, then you could talk for eight minutes on that subject. Would anybody like to volunteer to stand up and talk for eight minutes on what the speaker said?" Nobody ever does. But the worst is yet to come. When I say, "Does anybody remember *anything* the speaker said?" there is dead silence. Then the crowning blow is when I say, "Does anybody even remember the speaker's name?" I never cease to be amazed at the silence followed by laughter.

There is another aspect of visual aids that is more important than fun and games. Whatever our work, a significant piece of the job consists of persuading other people to a course of action we would like them to take. The bottom line is this: If you use visual aids, people are more likely to be persuaded to the course of action you would like them to take. And it also enhances the audience's perception of you. They will think you are better than you are. An average

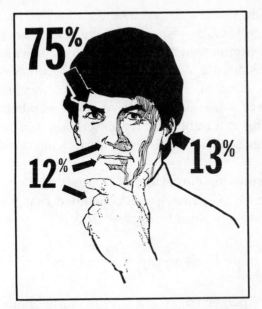

FIGURE 7A 75% of what we know came to us visually.

FIGURE 7B A picture is three times more effective than words and used together they are six times more effective than words alone.

presenter using visual aids can be more effective than a better presenter using no visuals—especially if the visuals are in color.

Visual aids stimulate interest in the subject, provoke thought, and clarify or substantiate what has been said. Moreover, when presented a new concept, the audience has no way of referring to a mental image of something they have never seen before.

If you're still in doubt, just try describing a camel to someone who has never seen a camel, without drawing a picture or using your hands.

Here's the smoking gun evidence. A study at the Wharton School of the University of Pennsylvania concluded that if you use visual aids (in this case overhead transparencies):

People are more likely to say "yes" and act on your recommendation.

You will be perceived as being more professional, persuasive, credible, interesting, and better prepared.

The probability of the audience reaching a consensus is 79 percent versus 58 percent without visual aids.

A similar study done at the University of Minnesota came to similar conclusions along with the startling revelation that people are 43 percent more likely to be persuaded if you use visual aids.

Before we get carried away, let's get back down to earth and remember that *you are still the center of the presentation*. Its success depends on how the audience perceives *you*. They must respect you, believe you, relate to you, and rely on you if you are to persuade them to a course of action you would like them to take. The good news is: Visual aids are your best friend to help make that happen. Listen to the words of a wise man.

I HEAR AND FORGET
I SEE AND I REMEMBER
I DO AND I UNDERSTAND
> *Kung Futse*
> *551–479 B.C.*

Kung Futse is his Chinese name. You know him better by his English name of Confucius.

Let's now cover some of the Do's and Don'ts of visual aids. The first three are the most important. Please pay particular attention to them.

- Keep it simple.
- Keep it simple.
- Keep it simple.
- No more than three curves on a graph. One or two are better.
- Do it in color. At least two, but no more than three.
- Have one and only one key point per visual. There is one exception: If the information is familiar to the audience you can combine a number of points.
- Don't have a page full of numbers.
- Translate complex numbers into pie charts or bar graphs.
- Don't use whole sentences or paragraphs—bullets only, please.
- Ask yourself this question: Can the audience quickly and easily grasp what they see?
- Use overlays for complex points.
- The world's worst visual aid is a black and white transparency of a typewritten page.
- Don't forget actual objects—the best visual aid is the real thing.
- If you can't have the real thing, have a picture of it.
- Do use pictures, graphs, and symbols.

The combined use of pictures, symbols, and key words create effective visuals to support the discussion of a key point or central thought.

Bar charts (either horizontal or vertical) are good for showing comparisons. Pie charts are good for showing the relationship of parts to a whole. Graphs are good for showing changes and trends over time. Diagrams are a good way to show complex structures or ideas.

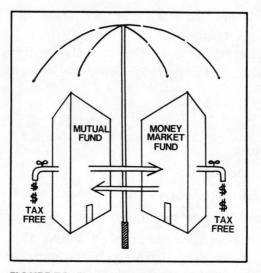

FIGURE 7C The most effective visual aids combine pictures, symbols, and key words.

Figure 7C is an example of a visual aid that combines pictures, symbols, and key words. The concept shown here is difficult to explain without a visual. But with a visual, the entire concept of switching funds under the tax-free umbrella of single premium variable life insurance becomes easy to explain and easy to understand.

The purpose of the visual aid is to focus attention and to accent and clarify the spoken word—not to do the presentation. We want the visuals to support the spoken word, not replace it.

Don't fail the test.

1. Is it simple?
2. Is it clear?
3. Is it visible?

Visual aids are even more effective in a presentation if you have a mix of charts, graphs, cartoons, bullets, overlays, and so on. This is particularly important in long presentations.

We suggested earlier that you not use visual aids that consist of complete sentences. Remember, the purpose of the visual is to support the explanation, not to give the explanation. Moreover, written material on visuals has the characteristic of poor retention. This is because reading is not really a visual aid. It is more like "hearing through the eyes." People will tend to remember the visual layout, not the message it contains. For example, they will remember that there was a bold heading and four subpoints, but not the content. Visual aids are most effective when they are *visual* in *impact* rather than verbal.

THE DESIGN OF VISUAL AIDS

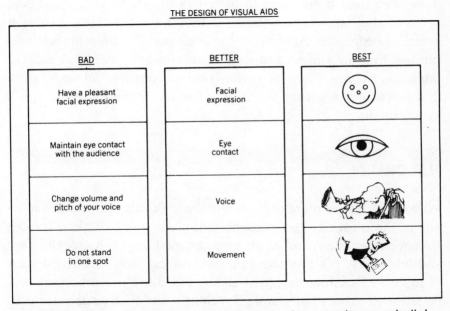

BAD	BETTER	BEST
Have a pleasant facial expression	Facial expression	
Maintain eye contact with the audience	Eye contact	
Change volume and pitch of your voice	Voice	
Do not stand in one spot	Movement	

FIGURE 7D Here we see the contrast between using a sentence, a bullet, or a picture as a visual aid.

If you are using words, use them in bullet form, not complete sentences. This gives the presenter the chance to elaborate on each point. The bullet word or words would then be an aid to the presenter.

Now we come to a deadly sin. Once you have been hooked on visual aids, the tendency is to reduce the entire presentation to a series of visuals. But they lose their effectiveness if you rely solely on them to get your message across. The more visuals you use, the less impact any of them will have. The natural tendency is to have far too many visuals. That's what causes Sin #6 of the Seven Deadly Sins: "Read verbatim every word on every visual." So don't cross the line. It's better to have too few than too many. If you plan on having too few, then you will be sure to concentrate the visuals on the key points.

One final general comment before we get specific about the details of making visual aids.

It's important that your visuals look neat, attractive, and well done. But they don't have to be works of art. In fact, it's almost better if they aren't. Sometimes if they have that slick look that smacks of Madison Avenue, it suggests that the presentation was put together for a mass audience of anonymous people. A presentation that has a touch of made-at-home conveys the impression that it was put together specifically for that audience and tailored just to them.

FLIP CHARTS

While high tech is marching on, the lowly flip chart continues to be one of the most effective presentation media of all, both as a main stream presentation and as an alternate medium to change the pace and add spice. It's also the most economical. You can invest a lot of money in custom-designed slides, but don't presume they will be more effective than simple flip charts. The best visuals are usually the simplest. They should enhance your presentation, not upstage it.

There is more good news about flip charts. They can't break down, they don't require electrical outlets or extension cords, and there are no bulbs to burn out. There is hardly anything that can go wrong with a flip chart presentation. It may be low tech, but it's high reliability.

And guess where your cheat sheet is? That's right, it's on the flip charts themselves, written lightly in pencil so the audience can't see. So the combination of the contents of the flip charts and the cheat sheet information gives you a shorthand script for the entire presentation. Just rehearse, and away you go.

"But wait," you say. "There's just one big problem with flip charts. *I'm not an artist.*" You don't have to be. Listen up.

Let's say you want to use pictures, drawings, or cartoons. First we need to find copies of originals we want to use. Don't worry about the physical size. We'll take care of that in a minute. Let me suggest three sources. The first is the *Yellow Pages.* Just look up the subject matter under the appropriate heading and 5 will get you 10 that you'll find a picture of what you want.

The second source is children's coloring books.

The third source is clip art. These are booklets of nothing but pictures, symbols, and cartoons. You can pick them up at an art supply store, or some office supply stores. Just ask for *clip art.* They will know what you're talking about.

The next step is to transfer the pictures, symbols, and cartoons we have selected to flip charts. The process is simple. First we make a transparency of the item. Then we place it on a projector and project it on to a blank flip-chart page. By moving the projector closer or further away we can get any size we want. Using a pencil, we now trace the projected image on to the flip-chart paper. The final step is to trace over our pencil marks with magic markers.

How about lettering? You will be surprised at how well you can do yourself with just a little practice and patience. A couple of tips will be helpful.

Use an 8½ × 11 piece of graph paper to plan the layout, establish the horizontal and vertical center lines, and position the lettering and the drawing in rough form. If you're into this in a big way, you can get a form from the supplier of flip-chart paper that does the same thing. It's called a flip-chart planning sheet.

Then select the flip-chart paper that has light blue lines on it for horizontal and vertical alignment. If you turn the paper over you can still see enough of the lines for printing alignment but they will not be visible to the audience.

In printing bullets a good rule of thumb is: No more than six lines, and no more than 8 to 10 words per page. Be sure to make them big enough for the audience. Letters that are one inch tall can only be seen easily from less than 15 feet away. Letters that are two inches tall can be seen from 30 feet. Better to have too big than too small. By the way, the light blue squares on the flip-chart paper are one inch in size.

Speaking of lettering and bullets, it's nice to have dots to the left of the bullets to set them off under the main heading. The problem comes in making them the same size with a magic marker. The first one looks just fine. But as you make the second one it becomes lopsided. In the process of correcting this it suddenly becomes bigger than the first one, and on and on goes the story. The simple solution is to buy stick-on dots. You can get them at an office supply store. They come in different colors and sizes.

If after giving this freehand lettering a shot you decide it's not for you, there are some back-up solutions. You can pick up plastic templates or dry transfer letters at an art supply store. Another solution is a mechanical arm device used by draftsmen. You put a magic marker in one end and trace out the lettering with a stylus on a template on the other end. The magic marker is positioned on the flip-chart paper, and BINGO—you have a professionally drawn letter. Again, check with an art supply store or audio-visual companies for this lettering set. Another solution is to ask around about lettering talent. Don't be surprised, for example, if it turns out that the teenage son or daughter of your next-door neighbor is a whiz at lettering.

Finally, if all of that fails, you can find talent at the local trade school or art school. You will find many students eager for some part-time work—especially art school students.

You know, of course, that we need to staple a blank sheet to each completed flip-chart page. If you don't, the contents of the page behind it will show through—just enough to be a bad distraction to the audience. If you don't staple the blank page, I promise you will forget there is a blank page and end up turning two pages for every one—and that's a distraction.

Here is something that will happen to you every time. You are almost through the presentation when someone says, "Can you turn back to X; I have a question about X." Now comes the problem of going backward through the charts trying to find "X." You will always miss it the first time through and end up turning all the charts back over, going through them at least one more time, and maybe more. I don't know how long that takes, but it always seems to me like an eternity. You can head this problem off at the pass by placing index tabs up and down the vertical side of the chart. Just cut out little pieces of a manila folder and Scotch tape them—get this—not to the page you want to turn to, but to the page in *front* of it. That way when you turn over the page with the tab, you have the right page showing.

You don't need a tab for every page, just those key pages you would expect to be asked about. This also makes an effective technique in a presentation if *you* want to refer back to a previous point you have established.

Before we leave the making of flip charts, just a couple of final points. Don't try to create a finished product the first time. You will find that it's off center, not vertically aligned, and so forth. Don't worry about it. This will be our rough draft chart. Just put a new page over it and redraw and reletter. It's easy to center and line things up by just moving the position of the top page. You will also notice an improvement in quality the second time around.

The chart maker's equivalent of hitting your finger with a hammer is misspelling a word on the last line of a chart. For some strange reason, it never happens at the top of the chart, always at the very bottom. Here's the solution. Lay the page on a pad of blank paper. Take a pen knife and cut out a small square or rectangle to remove the bad letter. If you press hard, you will also cut off a blank square or rectangle of exactly the same size in the blank page underneath. Having removed the square with the old letter, turn the page over and Scotch tape the blank square in the same spot from behind. It will fit exactly, of course, and even in the front row, they won't be able to see the repair work. You can now remake the correct letter on the new square.

To add pizzazz, interest, and attention to your presentation, you can create *overlays*. You do this by starting backward. That is, you create the final flip chart that has the total picture and details first. Then in front of it you simply have blank pages from which you have cut out sections to expose parts of the completed chart underneath. Using multiple cutout pages, you can sequentially reveal more and more of the completed chart. You can also color code each step of the revelation.

Another gimmick is to Scotch tape a second page to the bottom of a flip-chart page. This gives you a double-length page. You now have an expanded area to depict a roadmap-type concept, a flow of goods, or sequential steps. You can place the total picture before the audience. After the double-length flip-chart page is completed, you can cut just a couple of inches off the bottom of the second page. You can then fold it up and lightly tape it with masking tape. To solve the problem of tearing part of the paper off with the tape when you want to unfold it, do the following: Stick a small piece of masking tape permanently to the spot on the first page onto which you will be sticking the tape on the second page. That way you will be sticking masking tape on top of masking tape—and it works just fine. In fact, you can have multiple positions of tape down the page. This would allow you to reveal and talk about specific points while revealing them one point at a time. This can be very effective, but it's for small groups only, since a large group would not be able to see the bottom of the second page.

Another idea is to have actual cutouts of pie charts that you can hold in your hand to talk about, and then tape to a flip chart page that was designed for it.

In summary, if you take some blank pages, magic markers, patience, practice, and time, then stir well, you will end up with a feast fit for any audience.

We leave this subject on a high note with a new announcement. The single biggest disadvantage of flip charts has always been the wear and tear and dog-eared appearance after heavy use. Here's a high-tech solution. Have them laminated. That's right—the whole thing. Just look up laminations in the *Yellow Pages*. They'll fix you right up.

BLACKBOARD OR CHALKBOARD

We won't spend a lot of time on chalkboards—not because they're not effective, but because of limited availability.

If you know in advance that you will always have a chalkboard available, then you have an excellent opportunity. No other medium offers the space to show so much to so many at one time. It has many of the advantages of flip charts, but in addition it's horizontally continuous. So if you can write and talk (practice required) at the same time—and always have a chalkboard available—this may be your cup of tea.

It is the cup of tea for some of the world's best presenters: the faculty at the Harvard Business School. Their visual aid is almost exclusively the chalkboard.

The chalkboard is particularly good for showing the evolutionary development of a product, service, or chain of events. It's also effective where you are developing a concept or presenting a close that is dependent on establishing multiple key points along the way that are dependent on each other. The chalkboard allows you to visually reference back to previously established points in supporting and developing a new point.

The cheat sheets for a chalkboard presentation are a mirror image of what the blackboard will look like as you develop the presentation—with additional notes (like planted questions) for the presenter.

You need to have your own chalk or markers, and own your own eraser. More often than not there will be none of each in the room, so bring your own.

Please be aware that nothing requires as much planning, practice, and rehearsal as a chalkboard. The fatal flaw is running out of chalkboard before you run out of material. To keep that from happening requires a lot of practice.

OVERHEAD TRANSPARENCIES (FOILS)

Here it is: the all time winner of the popularity contest—and for good reason. If you were to list all the functional capabilities you would like to have in a visual aid medium, then ask the question, "Which one will be the most effective with the least effort at the most reasonable cost?", the hands-down winner is overhead transparencies.

The world of high tech allows you to be as sophisticated or as simple as you would like to be. You can have everything from multicolor, multifoil overlays graphically created by a computer with an on-line foil plotter and transmitted to you over phone lines from a remote location, down to simple but colorful transparencies made in three seconds on your own copier.

If you are going to play in the transparency ball game, let me save you a lot of time and trouble. Don't stumble and fumble and make the same mistakes others have made.

What you should do is invest a couple hours of your time and learn from the experts at no cost to you. In every major city one or more suppliers will offer a no-charge graphics or transparency workshop. This will save you lots of time and trouble. The tricks of the trade are a skill that is best learned in a workshop and not out of a textbook. Further, the state of the art is advancing rapidly. A workshop is the best way to get up-to-date.

To find a workshop in your city, turn to the *Yellow Pages* and look under "Audio-Visual." Check the ads. You may find a workshop mentioned in the ads. If not, call the companies with the larger ads and ask if they offer a workshop or training sessions on making transparencies. The ones that do are typically the suppliers that also offer the greatest variety of transparency material. That's what you are looking for—one-stop shopping for all your transparency supplies. In the workshop, you will get a working knowledge of how to make transparencies, how to use color, how to work with graphs, charts, and statistics. You will also learn the latest techniques and materials.

Creating a transparency presentation can be a low-budget operation. The vast majority of overhead transparencies are made by the user on his or her own copier or desk-top foil maker. Transparency material is manufactured to work in the place of paper in most copiers. The folks that run the workshops can fix you up with the right material for your copier.

We said earlier that the worst transparency is one that is made from a typed page. But if you use the typing ball element that goes by the name of "Orator" to create your original, you will have a size that is easily visible for small meetings. Then, instead of typing complete sentences, just type key words in a bullet format. Add a cartoon or appropriate drawing from a clip art book, the *Yellow Pages,* or even a simple stick-man drawing. Then copy the original onto a color (not black and white) transparency, and that's all there is to it.

The workshop folks can fix you up with a starter set. Some items to consider are:

- Pad of worksheets for designing transparencies
- Supply of various color transparencies
- Color adhesive film
- Billboarding film
- Color highlight write-on film
- Write-on film
- Felt-tip colored pens
- Dry transfer letters
- Frames
- Overlay hinges

Pad of Worksheets

These are worksheets specifically designed for laying out the transparency. They have a grid of light blue lines for vertical and horizontal alignment. In addition, there are centering lines for the page and a larger circle for a pie chart. These light blue guidelines will not show up when copied. The worksheets also provide guidelines to limit the size to $7\frac{1}{2} \times 9$ so that a frame can be used.

Colored Transparencies

With such a variety of beautiful colors available, there is no excuse for using black and white. Some suppliers even supply an assortment of colors within the same box. You can produce transparencies with black on colored background, colors on clear background, clear letters on colored background, and colored letters on different colored backgrounds. Some are designed to fit in a copier. The more exotic ones require a desk-top transparency maker.

Color Adhesive Film

This film comes in different colors and is ideal for coloring the different sections of a pie chart or bar chart. You stick it on the area you want covered, then remove the excess film after cutting out the exact pattern with a pen knife.

Billboarding Film

This is used to add a different colored background or border to a visual aid. You tape a sheet of the billboarding film over the entire transparency. Then, using a pencil knife, you cut around and remove the film over that part you want to billboard or stand out.

Color Highlight Write-on Film

Of all the different techniques, tricks, and gimmicks I have seen used, this is the one that provides the greatest impact. When people come up at the end of a presentation, usually the one thing they want to know is, "Where did you get that magic?"

Color highlight write-on film consists of a blue transparency with special chemicals in it so that when you write or draw on it with a special marker, the resulting effect is a brilliantly colored image of your writing or drawing. The image can be in several different colors, such as yellow, orange, or red. It's so brilliant that it looks like it would glow in the dark.

In addition to using it to write on or draw on, write-on film can also be overlaid on another transparency and used to highlight the printing underneath as you talk about it.

Write-on Film and Felt-tip Colored Pens

This is a kissin' cousin to the color highlight write-on film, except this film is clear and you write or draw on it using colored felt-tip pens.

This is an effective way of pencil talking, pencil drawing of concepts, or pencil filling-in-the-blanks.

Dry Transfer Letters

These come in different sizes and different styles. You can get them at your one-stop audio-visual or art supply store. They will add professional-looking lettering to your transparencies.

Frames

This is a good news, bad news subject. The good news is that frames block out the light around the edge of a standard size transparency and they are convenient for writing cheat notes to yourself. The bad news is that they are bulky and an odd size that does not fit well in most containers. They do not pack well for travel.

There is a new type of frame that overcomes the bad news and has an added advantage. It's called a flip frame. It's like a reusable transparent envelope inside which your transparency fits. It therefore provides protection against fingerprints, lint, and so on. It has flip panels on both sides that fold open when in use to provide the function of a frame and provide cheat sheet space. With the panels folded, punched holes along one edge permit convenient filing in a three-ring binder. If there is a disadvantage it's that you have to remember to flip open the panels and that you can't read your cheat sheet until the panels are open. Further, many presenters like to be able to look ahead and glance at their next cheat sheet. With the panels folded you can't do that. Without frames, you can stack your cheat sheet directly under its transparency. Then you can glance ahead and read the cheat notes through the next transparency.

Overlay Hinges

These are specifically designed to attach multiple overlays to a single frame.

An alternate technique I have used for years without frames is to have no attachment of one to another but to simply overlay one on top of another. Surprisingly, they are remarkably stable with no attachments. I do make an alignment mark in the upper corners of each transparency, however.

The three final things for us to discuss about transparencies are:

Lettering machines

The computer

Farming it out.

Lettering Machines

If you are going to be making a number of transparencies on a continuing basis, you might consider a lettering machine. They greatly reduce the time required to do lettering for transparencies. They produce perfectly aligned and spaced letters in a variety of typestyles and sizes.

The letters are keyed on a standard keyboard. The machine then produces the letters imprinted on a strip of Scotch tape. The tape is then stuck to the transparency worksheet and you are ready to copy and make the transparency. The clear tape will not show on the copy or the transparency.

The Computer

The single best method of creating transparencies is a personal computer with a quality graphics printer. So if you already have a PC, you're almost home. If you don't have a PC, do you have access to one through a friend, a business, a brother-in-law, or other source?

Next, we need a software package for graphics, symbols, and lettering. If you don't already have one, you should stop by a PC store. Tell them what you want. They have a variety of software packages. Your biggest job will be deciding which one is best for you. Ask to see a demonstration. You will find you can do lettering in different styles, in different sizes, and position it where you want it. In addition, there are inventories of graphic formats, pictures, symbols, and drawings with flexibility of size and position. Print out a few on the printer. The quality of the finished foil will be no better than the quality of the black and white original.

Of course you have to pay a piece of change for the software, but it's well worth it if you are going to be putting together a number of presentations over a period of time. On the other hand, if this is a one-shot deal, there are other alternatives, including the most painless of all, coming next.

Farming It Out

If all of this sounds confusing and too much like work, have I got a deal for you.

Let the other guy do it for you. In fact, before the sun goes down you can have a done deal. It'll be professionally done and in living color. The cost is not as great as you might think. So get on the phone. Let your fingers do the walking under the heading of Audio-Visual.

But you don't get off Scot-free. You have to do the basic design. What pictures? What words? Where? How big? The good news is that this can be in very rough form on a yellow pad. Just so the other guy can clearly understand what you want. He is a technician executing his skill, not a mind reader. So leave nothing to the imagination. If you spell it wrong, you get it back wrong—in living color.

SLIDES

Not long ago, slides were only for those with big bucks and weeks of patience!

But times have changed. As high tech marches on, the cost of slides has fallen dramatically. The wait time is now measured in a few days, instead of weeks. The key is shopping around. High tech has not fallen evenly on everyone. Some still follow the old ways with the old price and the old wait. On the other hand, there are those who can generate words and music on their color PC screen, take a picture of the screen, and give you a handful of slides before the first coffee break. In no other area of this business are price, quality, and service comparison more important. So do your homework. You won't get home free. But you will get home without paying the price of a limousine.

CHAPTER 8

Getting Attention And Keeping Interest

If you have flipped to this chapter first, you're in a good place. But please understand that no number of tips, tricks, or gimmicks on getting attention and keeping interest will make a good presentation out of one that has a bad foundation and poor structure. So charge straight ahead if you like, but before the whistle blows be sure to go back and read the chapter, Blueprint for Success. That's where we build the foundation and put up the structure.

The good news about attention and interest is that you've got a free ride for the first eight minutes. The bad news is, if you blow the first eight minutes, you're a dead duck for the rest of the hour or the rest of the day.

Almost always, the attention and interest levels are high at the beginning of a presentation. The audience is checking you out. "Is this going to be worth listening to?" "Is he or she any good?," or "Do I wish I had sat in the back near the door so I could sneak out?"

This is your great opportunity to capture the audience. The two mandatory things you must accomplish in the first eight minutes is a well thought out and comprehensive statement of your objectives, and a successful explanation of why it's in the audience's best interest to pay attention to what you have to say.

The problem is that even after a successful eight minutes, the high attention level cannot be maintained. The attention level will drift downward as the presentation progresses. Why is this? It simply has to do with the way we are. The human mind can comprehend at the rate of 600 words per minute. But most people speak at the rate of 150 to 200 words per minute. So there is a lot of idle time for the mind to drift and wander off to the beach or to wonderland. And when the mind wanders off to the beach it sometimes forgets to come back for the next word, or next sentence, or next hour.

Our job is to keep them off the beach. To do this we need to structure our presentation so that we add a touch of Hot Spice every six to eight minutes. The hot spice is an attention-getting device that is built into and becomes part of the presentation. It enhances, punctuates, and adds human interest to your presentation. Its purpose is to keep attention and interest at a high level by breathing some life into the presentation.

As presentations draw to a close, the presenter will almost always give the audience a hint that it's about over. You will hear phrases like:

"In summary . . ."

"In conclusion . . ."

"For my last transparency . . ."

"To wrap this up . . ."

What do you think happens to the attention level of the audience when they hear one of those phrases? That's right. It shoots up. It's about over. Wake up, Joe, it's coffee time.

The masters at capitalizing on this are people who make their livings with their mouths. And the world champions are politicians. Did you ever hear a politician use the phrases, "In conclusion," or "In summary" more than once within the same speech? Did they make a mistake and repeat themselves? Absolutely not. That phrase

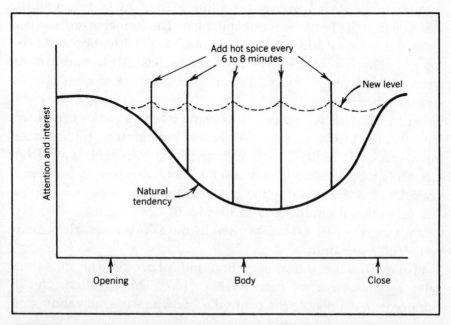

FIGURE 8A If we add Hot Spice we can overcome the natural tendency of the interest level to decline.

was carefully planted and spaced to keep the attention level of the audience as high as possible for as long as possible.

A close second to politicians was the preacher at the First Baptist Church in my hometown whose summary was almost as long as his sermon.

Before we jump into the specifics of adding spice, let's go back to those first eight minutes. We said that one of the things we must do in the first eight minutes is explain to the audience a selfish reason for them to pay attention to what you have to say. The consequences of not doing this are disastrous, and will guarantee a bad presentation.

Let's look at it this way. Suppose the material we would like to communicate is represented by the liquid in a pitcher. We would like to pour the material into a bottle (the audience). But the bottle has a stopper in it called, "What's in it for me?" Before we can get material into the bottle we have to remove the stopper. We remove the stopper by explaining a selfish reason for them to be interested.

Now we can pour the liquid into the bottle. But because the bottle has such a small opening, we spill as much over the sides as we get into the bottle. What we need is a funnel to allow us to get all the material into the bottle without spilling it. The funnel is represented by all the spice we add to the presentation to get attention and keep interest. The funnel is everything from eye contact to enthusiasm, from gestures to gimmicks. And the hottest spice of all is *you*. So let's talk about you.

Let me ask you a question. How many teachers and/or presenters have you seen in your entire life? From kindergarten, grade school, middle school, high school, college, Sunday school, Boy Scout school, Girl Scout school, computer school, seminars, training programs, and so forth? I don't know what the right answer is. Would you agree that it's in the area of 300 to 500?

If you agree with 300 to 500, then let me ask you this. How many were truly outstanding?

I have asked that question of thousands of people. The most common answers I get are two, three, or four. Think of that. Out of hundreds, most people can count the few who were outstanding on their fingers and have fingers left over.

That raises the question: What were the characteristics of the two,

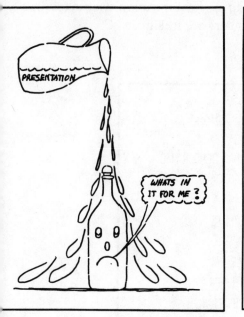
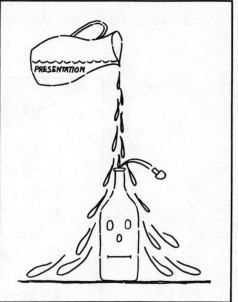
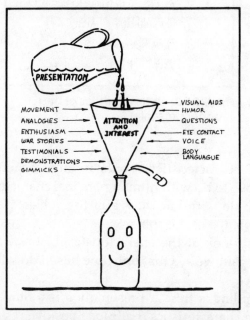

FIGURE 8B 1. The audience must have a selfish reason to pay attention.
2. A reason gets the plug out but most of the material spills on the floor.
3. Adding spice to get attention and interest is like adding a funnel.
Now all the presentation goes into the bottle.

three, or four who were outstanding? That question was asked in a study of 12,000 people. Their answers are in Figure 8C.

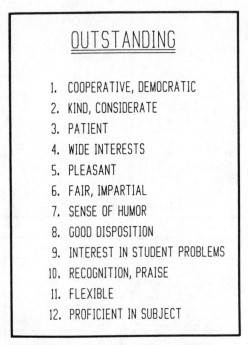

FIGURE 8C Characteristics of best teacher/presenter.

Of these 12 characteristics of outstanding teachers or presenters, how many have to do with human personal characteristics and how many have to do with knowledge of the subject? Only one has to do with knowledge of the subject.

We can also look at the characteristics of the worst teachers or presenters. Again we see that only one has to do with communicating the subject.

The bottom line is this: A presentation is a human relationship. Those human characteristics that cause positive results socially also create a positive attitude toward the presenter. People want to listen and learn from those whom they perceive as being sincere, warm, and friendly.

FIGURE 8D Characteristics of worst
teacher/presenter.

The intangibles of integrity, dedication, conviction, and concern are communicated 7 percent by our words, 38 percent by the way we speak, and 55 percent by our facial expression.

The audience is watching, listening, and saying, "Before I care how much you know, I want to know how much you care."

HUMOR

Of all the spice there is to use, the hottest spice of all is humor. Trouble is, very few of us are naturally humorous.

If someone who is not humorous tries to tell a joke, can you sense that it is awkward and unnatural? Yes, you really can. So the first rule of humor is don't tell jokes if it's not natural and comfortable.

There should be no doubt in your mind whether or not you are humorous. If you are, you know it very well. In fact, you have known it for years. It is obvious to both yourself and to the people around you. If there is any doubt in your mind, the answer is, you aren't.

The only thing worse than telling an awkward, unnatural joke is to tell a long, drawn-out awkward and unnatural joke. And yet, they do it every time.

Even the professional comedians back off from the long jokes. They learned long ago that the one-liner is best of all.

I know you've seen it many times. The speaker walks to the podium, whips out a prepared speech (which he didn't write), and proceeds to read verbatim, with a monotone voice and a solemn expression on his face, how excited he is to be here. (More about nonverbal expression later.) The very next thing he does is read a joke. And not just any joke. It's always a long joke.

Worse still, the joke has nothing whatsoever to do with the subject at hand. Which leads us to the second rule of humor: The humor must be relevant to the subject of the presentation. It's difficult enough for the audience to retain what you've said. Unrelated humor makes it worse. But natural humor that is directly related to the subject of the presentation will greatly enhance the material, its understanding, and its retention.

What do we do if we are uncomfortable telling jokes? Here's the answer: We tell stories on ourselves. Think back into your past. What we are looking for are situations, incidents, events, happenings, and experiences that at the time may have been embarrassing, stupid, humiliating, and so on. When you tell that incident or that experience you will tell it naturally, tell it with conviction, and tell it enthusiastically because it actually happened to you. So don't tell artificial jokes—tell the truth as it happened to you. Be sure it's tied-in and related to the point of the presentation you are trying to make.

There is an important and powerful by-product of telling stories on yourself. It enhances the audience's positive perception of you. People who tell stories on themselves are good people. Just be sure your stories are in the embarrassing category and not the boastful category. Otherwise, you'll get the opposite effect. All of us have embarrassing stories we can tell on ourselves.

For example: Many years ago when I was going through jet

fighter pilot training I was assigned to a pilot training base in Big Spring, Texas. The base has since been closed and only the old-timers remember that it was even there. Recently I was making a presentation in Texas. In the course of my remarks I mentioned that I had spent many months in Big Spring, Texas. At the end of the presentation the host came up to me and suggested that I should have explained what I was doing in Big Spring, Texas, since the only thing the audience knew about Big Spring was that it had an insane asylum and a prison—and they were wondering which one I had spent the many months in.

When I'm giving my corporate strategy presentation, I tell the story about my first visit to our corporate headquarters. I tell them that the thing that stood out most in my mind, more than anything else, was the color of the carpet.

"You would never guess the color of the carpet in our corporate headquarters. You would think it would be a pretty blue. But no. It's orange. That's right—orange. And not a pretty orange. It looks to me like the color of orange that would glow in the dark. I turned to the guy who was showing me around and said, 'Who in the world picked out this carpet?' He said, 'the President.'

"I immediately replied, 'Sure is pretty, isn't it?'"

Well, every time I tell that story to an in-house audience, it brings the house down.

Another way you can use humor is to capitalize on predictable things that will happen during a presentation. For example, it is predictable that one or more people will arrive late, that is, after you've started. If it fits your chemistry and your personality, you can use this as an opportunity for light humor. Think up and plan in advance what you would say, like "Come right in. Are you the one who does the time management lecture?" or "Come on in, I'm sorry we started early."

Of course, what you say not only needs to fit your personality but also the audience and its mood.

Another example: If you use transparencies without frames, it is predictable that sooner or later one of the transparencies will start floating and moving in some direction while laying on top of the projector. Knowing this, you can preplan what you are going to say when this happens, such as

"This subject is so hot it's hard to keep it in one spot."

"In spite of what you see, this is not a flaky, floating idea."

"This is so dynamic that it's moving, even as we sit here."

"This offer won't last long because it's on the move."

Another way to create humor is through the use of visual aids that have a built-in humor.

From birth to age 18, a girl needs good parents.
From 18 to 35, she needs good looks.
From 35 to 55, she needs a good personality.
From 55 on, she needs good cash.

Sophie Tucker, 1953

"OCTOBER"

"THIS IS ONE OF THE PECULIARLY DANGEROUS MONTHS TO SPECULATE IN STOCKS IN."

"THE OTHERS ARE JULY, JANUARY, SEPTEMBER, APRIL, NOVEMBER, MAY, MARCH, JUNE, DECEMBER, AUGUST, AND FEBRUARY."

– – – MARK TWAIN

FIGURE 8E Cartoons that relate to the subject are excellent sources of humor.

FIGURE 8F So are quotes.

EYE CONTACT

Have you been in of one those meetings where the presenter is looking at the floor, the ceiling, or out into space with a glazed look?

We speak to people through our eyes. Don't handicap yourself. Look at the audience. More specifically, look directly at one person in the audience for three to five seconds. Your goal should be to look directly at every person in the room at least once for three to five seconds.

Here's how. Before you speak the next sentence or thought, lock in on a specific person and hold that eye contact until you have completed that phrase or that thought. Careful now—not too long, because eye contact can turn into a stare and that can be intimidating.

If you have tent cards, name plates, or if you know the people or some of them, use their names as you speak to them.

If you just do these two simple things—make eye contact and use their names—I promise you, you will have no problem getting attention and keeping interest.

The best use of this technique I've ever seen is by the professors at the Harvard Business School. In the analysis of a case study, they will look at every person in the room multiple times and call them by name. And every person there thinks, "He's talking just to me." And he is—for those five seconds.

Let me tell you about a hidden danger. It happens to me all the time. In a typical audience there will be a few people who have big smiles on their faces and nod their heads yes to everything you say. Guess what the natural human tendency is? That's right, to look only at these people who are smiling and nodding yes.

Here's a story that illustrates the effect smiles from the audience can have on the presenter. At a university a particular professor had the annoying habit of racing back and forth across the front of the classroom. In this particular class, a large percentage of the students were from the same fraternity. They put together a plan back at the house. Here's what they did. When the professor reached a specific spot in his racing in front of the class, they would all smile. When he moved away from that spot they would stop smiling. Well, before that class was over, guess where the professor ended up standing? You got it—exactly on that spot where he got a lot of smiles.

There's a bonus for you if you concentrate on eye contact. It keeps you from turning your back on the audience and reading from a screen, a board, or a flip chart. You can't read a script *and* have eye contact with the audience. So lift up your head, smile, and look 'em in the eye.

VOICE

The first rule of the voice is to be heard. But don't confuse being heard with effective communications.

The single biggest problem with the voice is the tendency to speak in a monotone. And, in fact, if you are reading a script it's hard not to talk in a monotone. It takes a conscious effort to vary the volume, tone, and pitch of the voice.

A common mistake is to assume that all one has to do is speak in a loud voice. But an hour of loud monotone quickly becomes an hour of loud noise. In fact, just to illustrate the contrast, I have heard a 90-minute presentation made in a whisper. It was amazing. You could hear a pin drop. Everyone in the room was sitting on the edges of their seats, thinking at any moment the presenter was going to reveal the secret of the universe. An observer turned to me and said, "Did you know that people will believe anything if you whisper it?"

An effective use of the voice is the change of pace. Speak rapidly for a few seconds, pause, return to a normal pace, then speak rapidly again. The words per minute will average out to be the same as if you had spoken in a monotone, but what a difference. The master of this technique is Paul Harvey. In fact, if you want a free lesson on the use of the voice, just listen to the network anchor person on the evening news.

The antidote for the monotone is a mix of conviction, enthusiasm, confidence, desire, and rehearsal. Take a swig of that before you start, and you'll be in fine shape.

MOVEMENT

There is a psychological barrier that separates you from your audience. It's a line that runs across the front of the room—it's like the Berlin Wall. It creates the atmosphere of me/they, of we/them. It's like the offense versus the defense. It's an adversary relationship.

You need to break down that barrier—and it's easy to do. Just walk across the line occasionally. That says, "I'm one of you"; "I'm on your side"; "We're all in this together." Just a few steps forward into the audience will do it. If you're on a stage or a riser it's even more important to break the barrier by stepping down to ground level for a minute or two. If that's not practical, the least you can do is walk to the front of the stage.

Never underestimate the power of nonverbal communication. Use it to your advantage. What you *do* speaks louder than what you *say.* Walk across the line.

Be a triple-threat presenter. Have three positions, not one. The only thing worse than standing in one spot for an entire presentation is to be a racehorse running back and forth across the front of the room. That's a terrible distraction.

Here is the game plan. Position #1 is the home position for the mainstream part of your presentation. Position #2 is for the alternative media you will use to change the pace, add emphasis, and give the illusion of spontaneity. Decide in advance which material will be the mainstream media, and which will be the alternative. Be sure to use the alternative media at least once every 10 minutes.

Now in every presentation there are several places where you will elaborate in some detail on some point or concept. For some of these, you will know the subject so well and the words will flow so smoothly that you will have no need to refer to notes. That's the time to cross the line and break the barrier of the Berlin Wall. That's position #3. Again, decide in advance specifically when and where you will do this. Then rehearse. And do it the same way every time.

ANALOGIES

The way our minds work, we are better at understanding and remembering pictures and symbols than we are at remembering words. For example, when someone says the word *car,* our mind flashes up a mental picture of an actual car, not the English letters C-A-R. If I say *ice cream,* what image comes into your mind? I bet it's not letters of the alphabet.

The world's best communicators use analogies to create easy-to-understand images of their key points or concepts. So let's take a lesson from the pros. You can communicate concepts in less time, with better understanding, and with longer retention if you use analogies. They are so effective that people will remember some of them all their lives.

Have you ever seen a ski instructor teaching little children how to ski for the first time? To tell them how to slow down or stop, the instructor will say, "Make a snowplow with your skis." Or if they happen to be from the South where they have never seen a snowplow, the instructor will say, "Make a slice of pizza with your skis."

To teach them how to turn, the instructor might say, "Let's pretend that our knees are the headlights on a car. When a car turns, the headlights turn. Now place your hands on the headlights (knees). To turn to the right we simply turn the headlights (hands on knees) to the right, and so on."

Effective presenting is simply a matter of communicating the picture you have in your mind to the mind of another person. The more complex the material or concept, the more important it is to use analogies and word pictures. And the simpler, the better. For example, to explain what a computer program is, we could use the analogy of making a cake. To make a cake we follow a recipe. We do one step at a time in a predetermined sequence. A computer program is the same thing: a series of steps which, if followed in sequence, will lead to a predetermined result.

The most used analogy in my company for 30 years has been the analogy of an iceberg to explain our customer support—that part you don't see on the surface.

If you have trouble coming up with an analogy to explain some abstract concept, just explain it as best you can to your next-door neighbor, then ask him what it reminds him of. You will also find that barbers, bartenders, and taxi drivers will never fail to come up with an analogy.

THE REVELATION TECHNIQUE

To a large extent, if I can control what you see, I can control what you think.

The other side of the coin is, if I don't control what you see, then I lose control over what you think. For example, if I flash Figure 8H on a screen, and begin to discuss the first item, your eyes and your mind are reading ahead. You are not hearing what I'm saying about the first item because you are already halfway down the page.

LET ME TELL YOU ABOUT A STRATEGY

      ◉ IT'S EASY TO UNDERSTAND

LET ME TELL YOU ABOUT A STRATEGY

     ◉ IT'S EASY TO UNDERSTAND
     ◉ IT'S SIMPLE TO IMPLEMENT
     ◉ IT PROVIDES INSTANT LIQUIDITY
     ◉ IT REQUIRES LESS THAN ONE HOUR PER WEEK
     ◉ ALL ACTIVITY IS CONDUCTED BY PHONE
     ◉ YOU NEVER PAY SALES COMMISION
     ◉ IT'S IDEAL FOR IRA'S OR KEOGH PLANS
     ◉ IT DOES NOT REQUIRE YOU TO PREDICT, FORECAST, OR GUESS THE FUTURE
     ◉ IT MAKES MONEY IN GOOD TIMES AND IN BAD TIMES
     ◉ IT IS LOW RISK – HIGH REWARD

FIGURE 8G The revelation technique allows me to control your thinking by controlling your seeing.

FIGURE 8H Here I have lost control over what you are seeing and hence what you are thinking.

As a presenter, I must not let that happen. I want you to read the item halfway down the page only when I am ready to talk about it.

The way I control this is the revelation technique. Let's suppose I am using an overhead projector. Using a blank piece of paper I simply cover up the transparency, revealing the items one at a time as I discuss them, as in Figure 8G.

Variations of this technique are effective for a step-by-step explanation of a concept. Figure 8I illustrates a four-step revelation to explain true interest rates. Please note, this is not a series of over-

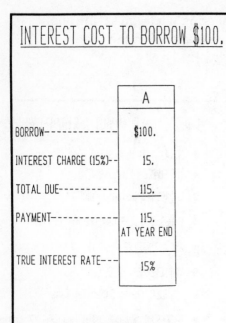
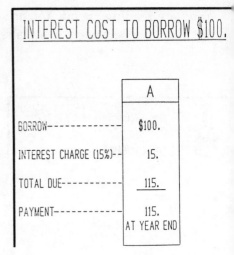

INTEREST COST TO BORROW $100.

	A
BORROW------------	$100.
INTEREST CHARGE (15%)--	15.
TOTAL DUE----------	115.
PAYMENT-----------	115. AT YEAR END
TRUE INTEREST RATE---	15%

INTEREST COST TO BORROW $100.

	A
BORROW------------	$100.
INTEREST CHARGE (15%)--	15.
TOTAL DUE----------	115.
PAYMENT-----------	115. AT YEAR END

INTEREST COST TO BORROW $100.

	A	B
BORROW------------	$100.	$100.
INTEREST CHARGE (15%)--	15.	15.
TOTAL DUE----------	115.	115.
PAYMENT-----------	115. AT YEAR END	9.50 PER MONTH
TRUE INTEREST RATE---	15%	

INTEREST COST TO BORROW $100.

	A	B
BORROW------------	$100.	$100.
INTEREST CHARGE (15%)--	15.	15.
TOTAL DUE----------	115.	115.
PAYMENT-----------	115. AT YEAR END	9.50 PER MONTH
TRUE INTEREST RATE---	15%	27%

FIGURE 8I The revelation technique can be used to reveal a little at a time or a lot at a time.

lays—it is simply covering up with blank paper what you do not want to reveal until you are ready to talk about it.

This allows you to control the attention and focus the thought process through a series of logical steps to a conclusion.

The final transparency without this technique would be confusing and difficult to explain. You would have no control over which part of the transparency your audience is looking at and what they are thinking. Certainly you would lose the element of surprise.

NUMBERS AND STATISTICS

A sure way to lose the attention and interest of your audience is to start showing a bunch of numbers and statistics. And yet many times these numbers are the very foundation of the key point you are trying to make.

What to do?

The first rule is: no pages full of numbers. A better way is to show numbers using graphs, bar charts, or pie charts.

But what if the nature of the numbers and the points we are trying to make don't lend themselves to a graph? Here are some thoughts on how to present numbers.

Extract from a page of numbers a few of the key numbers, then develop a visual aid that builds a story around these numbers.

Take a look, for example, at Figures 8J AND 8K. One is a page full of numbers. The other shows the journey of a two-year-old child through life. That's the difference between a textbook and a romantic novel. From the audience's point of view, that's the difference between a turn-off versus a turn-on.

Another example might be to replace a page full of statistics showing sales volumes for the last 10 years with a few numbers illustrating that for the last 10 years the fastest growth has occurred during periods of new product introductions.

Another way of handling numbers is to organize them in such a way that they will not only prove your point, but invite audience participation and an element of surprise.

In Figure 8L, the audience is asked whether they would rather have their money in investment "A" or investment "B" for five

$1,000.
20% COMPOUND GROWTH RATE

YEAR	START OF YEAR	END OF YEAR	AVERAGE ANNUAL RETURN
1	$1,000 + 20% =	$1,200	20%
2	1,200 + 20% =	1,440	22%
3	1,440 + 20% =	1,728	24%
4	1,728 + 20% =	2,073	26%
5	2,073 + 20% =	2,488	29%
6	2,488 + 20% =	2,985	33%
7	2,985 + 20% =	3,583	36%
8	3,583 + 20% =	4,299	41%
9	4,299 + 20% =	5,159	46%
10	5,159 + 20% =	6,191	51.9%

FIGURE 8J A page full of numbers. A textbook. A turn-off.

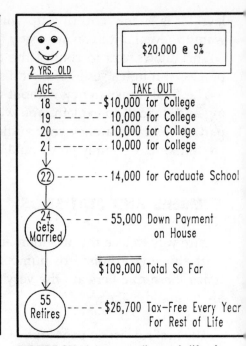

FIGURE 8K A journey through life. A romantic novel. A turn-on.

years. Which would you choose? Most people chose investment "A," which, of course, is the wrong choice. For every $1000 invested over five years, you would have ended up with $1485 in investment "A," but $1762 if you had put your money in investment "B."

So if you use numbers, create a story to go with the numbers. Then remove all numbers that don't contribute to the story. If you do that you'll have it just right.

HUMAN INTEREST

A sure way to keep interest is to appeal to human interest.

A good example is to tell the inside story. If you can start a sentence with, "The first thing I noticed about the Oval Office was . . .," you've got them in the palm of your hand.

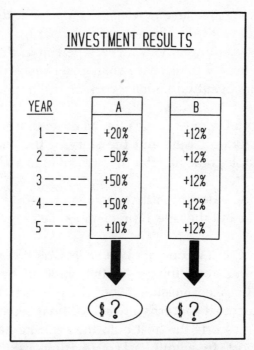

FIGURE 8L The organization of numbers can invite participation and cause surprise. The better choice is "B."

Not all of us have been in the Oval Office, but all of us have the inside story on something.

"What really happened on that day?"

"What is he or she really like?"

"How was the decision really made to buy X, do Y, or change to Z?"

People like things that are different, unusual, or a change of pace. The popularity of Trivial Pursuit is no accident. For example, in some of my presentations I use a rustic, crooked stick for a pointer. I have a trivial (but true) story that goes with the stick. It concerns:

Where I found it—Joyce Kilmer National Park.

What's different about that—largest stand of virgin timber in the eastern United States.

Who was Joyce Kilmer?—a writer and a poet.

Was Joyce Kilmer a man or a woman?—a man; he died in his early twenties on a battlefield in France in World War I.

He left us something of which every person in the room knows the first two lines: "I think that I shall never see/A poem as lovely as a——," and a beautiful national park of virgin timber in western North Carolina.

The curiosity of people in such things never ceases to amaze me. Often to save time, I leave out the story of the stick. Invariably, when I do, people come up after the presentation and ask me about the stick.

An interesting sidelight is that years later, people will have forgotten my name but they always remember me as the man with the stick.

The popular PBS TV program *Wall Street Week* has as its guest the heavy-hitters and deep-thinkers of the world of finance. But the most frequently asked question about the program concerns none of these big names. It concerns a woman who is seen only for a few seconds as she escorts the host onto the set. She never says anything. The most frequently asked question is, "Who is that woman?"

I'll never forget a presentation made by a colleague of mine. He was told that this would be an important meeting of important people and this should be a formal presentation. So at the appointed time he walks in dressed in (guess what?) a tux—complete with tails and a top hat. Well, let me tell you, no one in that meeting will ever forget that *formal* presentation.

Not many of us would feel comfortable pulling that off. But all of us can breathe life into our presentations by using human interest stories or trivia that are personal to us.

Another variation of human interest is the use of human interest *questions*. Figure 8M is a questionnaire concerning the abuse of credit. You can hear a pin drop when I show that questionnaire on the screen. I conceal the answer at the bottom using the revelation technique, and reveal it after a long pause when everyone has finished the questions.

People will pay attention and be interested when the subject directly pertains to them and their well-being. Human interest ques-

THE FLASHING RED LIGHT EXAM

o DO YOU SPEND MORE THAN 20 PERCENT OF YOUR TAKE-HOME PAY ON MONTHLY INSTALLMENT BILLS, NOT INCLUDING MORTGAGE PAYMENTS?

o DO YOU REGULARLY RECEIVE "SECOND NOTICES."

o HAVE YOU RECENTLY BORROWED CASH WITH YOUR CREDIT CARD TO MEET HOUSEHOLD EXPENSES?

o DO YOU FIND IT IMPOSSIBLE TO PUT MONEY INTO A SAVINGS ACCOUNT?

o ARE YOU CURRENTLY BEING TELEPHONED BY A BILL COLLECTOR.

o DO YOU SECRETLY SUSPECT THAT YOUR CREDIT CARD SPENDING HAS GOTTEN OUT OF CONTROL?

o ARE YOU WORRIED ABOUT YOUR DEBTS?

o IS THERE FREQUENT STRESS AT HOME BECAUSE OF OVERDUE BILLS?

IF YOU ANSWERED "YES" MORE THAN ONCE, THEN THE RED LIGHT IS FLASHING FOR YOU.

FIGURE 8M People will pay attention if the subject pertains to them and their well-being.

tions not only get attention, they are also a dramatic way of making your point.

MAKE IT ALIVE, REAL, AND CURRENT

If you use references or quotes, consider a picture of the individual and a tidbit or two of human interest information.

For example, in talking about the profile of a millionaire, I introduced the subject by saying, "I want you to meet the richest man in America." (Show transparency picture.) "His name is Sam Walton. He owns the Wal-Mart Stores. He lives in Bentonville, Arkansas, population 9,920, drives a pick-up truck, and has breakfast at the Daylight Donut Shop."

Nobody ever went to sleep while being introduced to the richest man in America.

It's easy to make a transparency from a picture in a magazine or newspaper. First make a copy on the copier, then make the transparency from the copy. Works like a charm.

Something else that will impress your audience is to show and use references or examples that are hot off the press, such as current articles from *The Wall Street Journal*, the local paper, or current magazines.

An attention-getting technique is to cut out the article and make a transparency out of it. How's that for showing how much you're on top of the subject? And it gives the audience the feeling that they are in-the-know with the latest scoop.

HOW TO STAY AWAKE DURING A FILM

Even the best can lose an audience during a film.

How do we keep them awake during this traditional snooze time? More importantly, how do we insure that they get from the film the reason for showing it?

Here's how.

First, before showing the film, give the audience a preview of

FIGURE 8N Use articles and quotes that are hot off the press.

what it's about. Second, tell them what to watch for in the film. Third, tell them what questions we will discuss about the film when it's over.

Here's one of the cleverest things I have ever seen. A presenter in introducing a film suggested that the audience pay particular attention to the very last line, since that was the key to the entire film and would be the subject of discussion at the end of the film.

Well, have you ever tried to watch and listen for the last line in a film? Problem is, you never know when it's coming. Especially if you don't know how long the film is. Every line could be the last line.

Is that sneaky? Maybe so, but it sure keeps them awake.

HANDOUTS

Let's talk about handouts. Are they friend or foe? Should they be distributed at the beginning or at the end?

Handouts, if properly used, can greatly enhance audience attention and interest. On the other hand, if not properly used, they can more than detract—they can cause you to lose the audience.

Whether or not to have a handout depends on the subject, your objective, the complexity of the material, and the expected use of the information.

The most common approach to handouts is to simply reproduce a copy of all the visual aids and distribute them at the beginning of the presentation. If you do this you are almost sure to lose the audience. You have just created an environment for a heads-down audience. You have lost the effect of your strongest and most important visual aid—yourself. Worse still, the audience, instead of being *with* you, will tend to be a visual aid or two *ahead* of you.

What to do? What *not* to do is to distribute a complete copy of the handout in advance. Yet there can be certain material like a flow chart or a schematic diagram for which a handout would be helpful. It would allow the audience to make notes directly on the handout.

Here's a suggested way of handling that. Typically, in an hour's presentation, there would not be more than three or four handout sheets that would truly be helpful for note taking. Make separate copies of these and distribute them individually only when you come to that subject in the presentation. Additional handout material should be distributed at the end of the presentation. A convenient and painless way of handling this is to stack the handouts on a table near the door so your audience can pick up a copy on the way out.

Are there any exceptions to this? There sure are.

Suppose I distributed a complete set of handouts in advance, but when you looked at the handout and flipped through it, there was nothing on it. Every page looked something like Figure 80.

The handout consisted of nothing but a bare-bones outline of a format with most of it blank. One look at this and the audience quickly understands that there is no point in looking ahead because there is nothing to see.

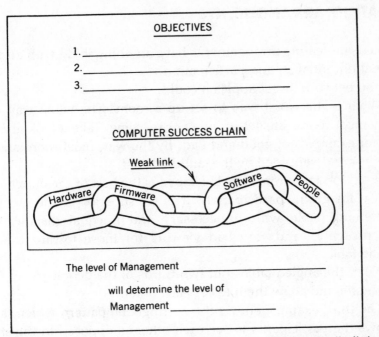

FIGURE 80 A good handout. They hear, they see, they write it down.

But now watch what happens. I project the first overhead on the screen. As I speak about the content I fill in the blanks by writing directly on the transparency with a felt-tip pen. And so, using key words, I complete the session objectives, I write "management involvement" on the unnamed link of the chain, and I fill in the blanks for the statement at the bottom so it will read, "The level of Management *involvement* will determine the level of Management *satisfaction*."

What do you think the audience is doing with their copies of this handout as I am filling in the blanks? That's right. They are also filling in the blanks.

And so we have created the perfect environment for people to learn, understand, and retain. In the words of Confucius, they hear it, they see it, and they do it.

SEATING ARRANGEMENTS

Could the seating arrangements have anything to do with audience attention, interest, and participation?

You bet your sweet apples it could.

What is the worst way to set up a room? The worst way is the way most rooms are set up most of the time. Take a look at Figure 8P for examples of good and bad. By the way, most room arrangements are determined by the janitorial staff.

From top to bottom: The U-shaped is the best of the bunch when you want group participation. It is far superior to the elongated conference table with unnecessary and unequal distance from the presenter, and very bad viewing for those toward the back of the table.

Next, the angled tables put two-thirds of the people closer to the presenter and allow them to see each other.

The third example shows the herringbone pattern which, again, allows the participants to see each other as opposed to the stereo-typed classroom arrangement.

The final example shows an amphitheater or horseshoe seating arrangement as opposed to a military formation. Again, not as formal, more open, able to see others, and more conducive to participation.

Generally, wide and flat is better than narrow and deep.

If there are windows in the room, arrange it so that it is the presenter who can look out the windows, not the audience. And don't have a clock in view of the audience.

CONVICTION AND ENTHUSIASM

We close this chapter by listing the characteristics of good presenters and some of the techniques they use to get attention and keep interest.

There is one ingredient that we have not talked about. It is the most important of all. So important is it, that there is nothing that is a close second. With this ingredient you can forget all others.

ROOM ARRANGEMENTS

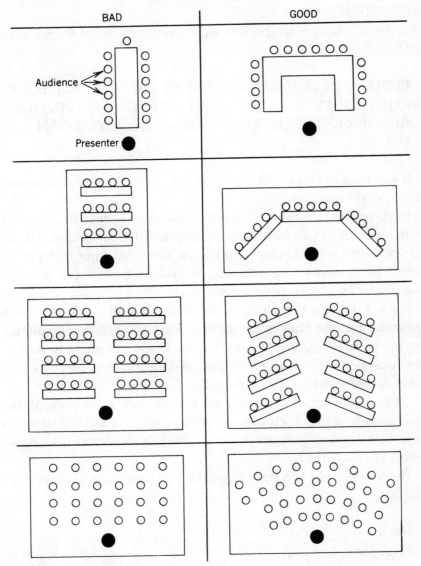

FIGURE 8P The worst way to set up a room is the way most rooms are set up most of the time.

Without it, you need all the help you can get. The magic ingredient is ENTHUSIASM.

There is a simple truth I learned from people wiser than myself. It's this:

PEOPLE ARE PERSUADED MORE BY THE DEPTH OF YOUR CONVICTION THAN THE HEIGHT OF YOUR LOGIC, MORE BY YOUR ENTHUSIASM THAN ANY PROOF YOU CAN OFFER.

If you believe you could use some help in the area of enthusiasm, let me share two thoughts.

First, you should ponder your own belief and depth of conviction in the subject. If you have doubts, reservations, or conditional allegiance to the subject, then you should not be making that presentation. So do some soul searching or find another subject to which you can make a total commitment.

Second, I ask you to think of the audience in this context. If you are making a one-hour presentation to 40 people, then you are taking up 40 hours of other people's time. If you are going to take up the equivalent of one week of your audience's time, then they deserve the very best you've got to give.

Or look at it this way. If you are giving a one-hour presentation to 40 people, and if their average annual salary is $60,000, then the collective value of that one hour is $2400. Is what you have to say worth $40 a minute?

The thought of $40 a minute will get my juices flowing real good, real fast.

The Good Presenter

Objectives clearly stated

Develops interest in the subject

Logical flow

Material is current

Correct level of detail

Stimulates questions

Good visual aids

Good appearance

Pleasant and varied voice

Creativity

Positive body language

Gestures

Movement

Analogies

Confidence

Conviction

Credibility

Integrity

Dedication

Sincerity

Concern

Smile

Eye contact

Varied pace

Starts on time

Ends on time

Summarizes key points

Achieves objectives

CHAPTER 9

Samples Of Hot Spice

If you've been wondering what all this Hot Spice looks like or tastes like, here are a dozen or so samples that fall into the general category of fun and games. For some they will be too much fun and too much of a game. That's alright, don't force-fit something that's unnatural and uncomfortable for you.

Other powerful categories of Hot Spice are more directly related to the material of your presentation—categories like questions, analogies, war stories, testimonials, and so on.

What's the best Hot Spice? The best is none of the above but all of the above. By that we mean a mixture of several different categories.

Remember, it is important that we tie in the Hot Spice to the subject. If you can do that it's a sure-fire way of making your point, having it understood and remembered. If you're interested in doing well and having the audience say, "That was a great presentation," then you need some Hot Spice. That's what will breathe life, humor, and excitement into your presentation. It will make the difference between plain vanilla and a banana split.

How much do we need and how often do we need it? Well, we don't need it during the opening or the close. Remember, the audience level is already high during the opening. Further, we have specifically designed the close to be the high point of the presentation, so we don't need help there. If we can count on good audience attention during the first 10 minutes of the opening and the 5 minutes of the close, then that will leave us 45 minutes in a one-hour presentation that needs Hot Spice.

Figuring a shot of spice every six to eight minutes, that means we need six or seven shots.

To get six or seven shots of Hot Spice, we need an inventory of around 25 to 30 to choose from. You will find that with a little creativity and imagination you will be able to adapt about one out of every four to some key point of your presentation.

A good idea is to set yourself up a Hot Spice file. Then as you run across cartoons, jokes (that fit your chemistry), games, gimmicks, tricks, and so on, just drop them in your spice file. That makes it easy to pick and choose from an inventory and fit the spice to the presentation.

If your needs are immediate and you don't have an inventory of spice, just go to the magazine stand in the larger book stores. There in the general area of crossword puzzles you will find a magazine by the name of *Games*. It's Hot Spice from cover to cover.

Jokes and stories are examples of Hot Spice, but they need to fit your chemistry. In fact, you need to feel natural and comfortable with all the spice you use. For example, not everyone would feel comfortable doing the following:

- Crumpling up speech notes and throwing them on the floor (even though they're blank paper).
- Throwing a ball to someone in the audience.
- Doing a magic trick.
- Pouring water to overflow a glass.
- Setting off a firecracker.
- Guessing the number of jelly beans in a glass and relating the number to a point you're making.

Figure 9A is a five-question test which I give verbally to the audience. The key is to do it rapidly and not give them a lot of time to think. When it's over, I tell them that the correct answers (with tongue-in-cheek) are red, rose, chair, Three, and Lion.

I then ask for a show of hands of those that got three or more correct, then four or more correct, then all five correct.

```
WHAT IS YOUR FAVORITE COLOR ?

NAME A FLOWER.

NAME A PIECE OF FURNITURE.

PICK A NUMBER FROM 1-4.

NAME AN ANIMAL IN A ZOO.
```

FIGURE 9A The behavior of an audience can be predicted. The most common answers are: red, rose, chair, three, and lion.

Typically, over half the audience will get three or more correct, some 25 percent will get four or more correct, and a number will get all five correct. Well, the laws of probability would say that the odds of this happening are a zillion to one—and yet it happens every time.

I then reveal that in studies that have been done, those happen to be the most frequent answers to those five questions.

I use this to illustrate that given the right circumstances, the behavior or reaction of an audience can be predicted.

Figure 9B is a transparency I show on the screen. I explain that these are the letters of the alphabet in two lines—except I forget to put the "Z" in. Does the "Z" go in the top line or the bottom line? I ask them to raise their hands when they know the answer.

A E F H I K L M N T V W X Y

B C D G J O P Q R S U

WHICH LINE WOULD THE "Z" GO ON ?

FIGURE 9B Look at the big picture—not the details. The correct answer is the top line. All letters on the top line are made with straight lines.

It becomes obvious to the audience that very few raise their hands. I then explain that the "Z" goes on the top line since the common denominator of the top line is that every letter is made up of straight lines whereas every letter on the bottom line has a curve in it.

I use this to illustrate the point that you have to know what to look for, or you will never find the right answer.

Take a look at Figure 9C. "Let's see if we can identify famous people just by their hair styles."

FIGURE 9C You don't have to know all the details to come to the right conclusion.

The answers are: Princess Di, Ronald Reagan, Captain Kangaroo, Albert Einstein, George Washington, Bo Derek, Elvis Presley, Farrah Fawcett, Groucho Marx, and William Shakespeare.

This can be used to illustrate that you don't have to know all the details to come to the right conclusion, or that some characteristics dominate all others.

If I wanted to talk about something important that was going to happen on Tuesday, I might introduce the subject with the piece of spice shown in Figure 9D.

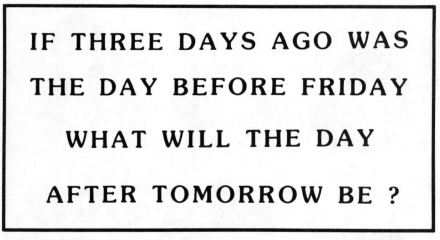

FIGURE 9D Example of hot spice to focus attention on a specific day.

By changing the word *Friday* I can cause the right answer to be any day I want it to be.

If I wanted to illustrate how easy it is to make a change I might show the roman numeral IX and ask the audience to make it a 6 with one stroke of the pen.

The answer is to put an "S" in front of it so that it looks like this: "SIX."

This can also be used when you are talking about six of anything or nine of anything. Or it can be used to illustrate the power of a stroke of the pen.

Here's one that's a lot of fun. You can use it to show how you can be tricked with numbers, how some people can prove anything with numbers, or a play on the old adage of, "Figures don't lie, but liars figure."

Ask the audience to take the change out of their pockets or purses.

- Count it (Maximum of two digits)
- Double it
- Add 5
- Multiply by 50
- Add 1526
- Add America's age (America's age was 211 in 1987)
- Subtract the year of your birth

The first two digits will be the change you started with. The last two digits will be your age.

Figure 9E never ceases to amaze me. Whenever I use it people start writing down those words.

You can use it to talk about the power of words. For example, when a large national retailer wanted to break into the plastic credit card business they chose one of these words as the name of their credit card.

Speaking of words, the most powerful word combinations in the English language are shown in Figure 9F.

Here's something different. If you are going to reference an event or date in history, you can get copies of the *New York Times* on any date since 1851.

It's interesting to relate what else was going on in the world on a particular date that is important in your presentation.

A variation of this is to get newspapers made up with a fake headline that pertains to your subject, to this particular meeting, or to someone on the program or in the audience.

Figure 9G is an all-purpose piece of Hot Spice. Your imagination is your only limitation.

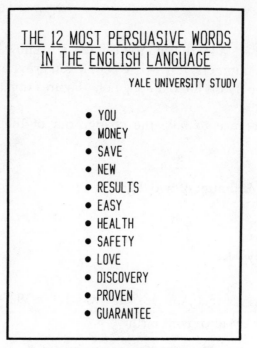

FIGURE 9E Powerful single words.

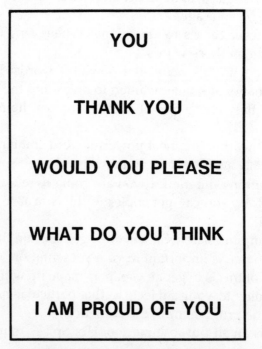

FIGURE 9F The most powerful word combinations in the English language.

1. <u>MAN</u>
   BOARD

7. <u>GROUND</u>
   FEET
   FEET
   FEET
   FEET
   FEET
   FEET

2. <u>STAND</u>
   I

8. <u>MIND</u>
   MATTER

3. R/E/A/D/I/N/G

9. HE'S/HIMSELF

4. <u>WEAR</u>
   LONG

10. DEATH/LIFE

5. T
   O
   W
   N

11. GESG

6. <u>0</u>
   M.D.
   PHD.
   DDS.

12. CYCLE
    CYCLE
    CYCLE

FIGURE 9G All-purpose spice. Answers are on the next page

IN EACH GROUP OF 5, 4 OF THE PEOPLE LISTED HAVE SOMETHING
IN COMMON AND THE 5TH ONE IS THE ODD ONE OUT. WHO?

RICHARD NIXON   MARILYN MONROE
LYNDON JOHNSON   RAQUEL WELCH
HARRY TRUMAN   SUZANNE SOMERS
CALVIN COOLIDGE   LONI ANDERSON
DWIGHT EISENHOWER   JAYNE MANSFIELD

STEVE MARTIN   PETER PAN
LOU COSTELLO   CHARLIE BROWN
ANN MEARA   RUDOLPH (REINDEER)
GRACIE ALLEN   WOODSTOCK (PEANUTS)
STAN LAUREL   SUPERMAN

SIGMUND FREUD   EDGAR ALLAN POE
JOHN F. KENNEDY   ELLERY QUEEN
AYATOLLAH KHOMEINI   GEORGE SAND
ABE LINCOLN   GEORGE ELIOT
WALT WHITMAN   O. HENRY

ANSWERS:

EISENHOWER WAS NEVER VICE PRESIDENT

RAQUEL WELCH IS NOT BLOND

MARTIN IS A SINGLE COMIC

CHARLIE BROWN CANNOT FLY

KENNEDY DID NOT HAVE A BEARD

POE IS HIS REAL NAME, OTHER ARE PEN NAMES

FIGURE 9H More all-purpose spice.

ALL ANSWERS END IN "GO

1. ILLINOIS CITY
2. ONE OF THE BEATLES
3. WALT KELLY'S CARTOON POSSUM
4. "IT TAKES TWO" DANCE
5. BLUISH COLOR OF THE SPECTRUM
6. SIGN OF THE ZODIAC
7. PINK TROPICAL BIRD
8. FRIEND, SOUTH OF THE BORDER
9. "LES MISERABLES" AUTHOR
10. PREVIOUS NAME FOR ZAIRE
11. KIND OF CUBAN DRUM
12. SAMOAN PORT
13. CLUSTER OF ISLANDS
14. FREUDIAN CONSCIENCE
15. JUICY TROPICAL FRUIT
16. SHIP'S LOAD
17. 1958 HITCHCOCK THRILLER
18. NORTH DAKOTA CITY
19. PAINFUL RHEUMATISM OF THE ABDOMEN
20. TRADE RESTRICTION

1. CHICAGO
2. RINGO
3. POGO
4. TANGO
5. INDIGO
6. VIRGO
7. FLAMINGO
8. AMIGO
9. VICTOR HUGO
10. CONGO
11. BONGO
12. PAGO PAGO
13. ARCHIPELAGO
14. SUPEREGO
15. MANGO
16. CARGO
17. VERTIGO
18. FARGO
19. LUMBAGO
20. EMBARGO

FIGURE 9I People like fun and games and mind teasers. Here is a warm-up
for a close (along with the answers) when you're asking the audience to
GO-TEAM-GO.

The correct answers to Figure G are:

1. Man overboard. 2. I understand. 3. Reading between the lines. 4. Long underwear.
5. Downtown. 6. Three degrees below zero. 7. Six feet underground. 8. Mind over matter.
9. He's beside himself. 10. Life after death. 11. Scrambled eggs. 12. Tricycle.

Here's a story I use that illustrates how people misunderstand what they read.

Show the first transparency shown in Figure 9J(1) for a few seconds. Then turn it off and ask the audience to take the True/False quiz in Figure 9J(2) on what they just read.

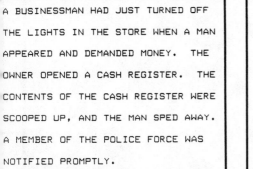

A BUSINESSMAN HAD JUST TURNED OFF THE LIGHTS IN THE STORE WHEN A MAN APPEARED AND DEMANDED MONEY. THE OWNER OPENED A CASH REGISTER. THE CONTENTS OF THE CASH REGISTER WERE SCOOPED UP, AND THE MAN SPED AWAY. A MEMBER OF THE POLICE FORCE WAS NOTIFIED PROMPTLY.

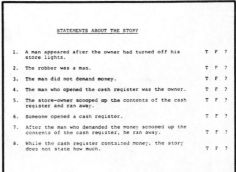

STATEMENTS ABOUT THE STORY

1. A man appeared after the owner had turned off his store lights.   T F ?
2. The robber was a man.   T F ?
3. The man did not demand money.   T F ?
4. The man who opened the cash register was the owner.   T F ?
5. The store-owner scooped up the contents of the cash register and ran away.   T F ?
6. Someone opened a cash register.   T F ?
7. After the man who demanded the money scooped up the contents of the cash register, he ran away.   T F ?
8. While the cash register contained money, the story does not state how much.   T F ?

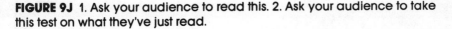

FIGURE 9J 1. Ask your audience to read this. 2. Ask your audience to take this test on what they've just read.

Figure 9K can be used to illustrate the importance of understanding the principle and logic behind an objective you're trying to achieve.

We pass out a sheet of paper with Figure 9K on it. We instruct the audience to take a pencil or pen and draw a line connecting the numbers in sequence starting with the number "1."

After 15 or 20 seconds we ask them to stop where they are. We then ask for a show of hands of those who ended up on a number greater than 15, then greater than 20, then greater than 25, and so forth. We then ask those with the highest numbers why they did so well. Typically we will find that they discovered the simple secret that the numbers alternate in sequence back and forth between the left and right hand side of the page.

Here's one that will leave them with their mouths open.

Explain that you are going to demonstrate your extrasensory perception (ESP).

FIGURE 9K With a pen or pencil, connect the numbers in sequence starting with the number "1." How far did you get in 20 seconds? Did you find the secret?

Ask for a volunteer to come to the front and write any three-digit number on the flip chart. Position yourself off to the side and slightly behind the flip chart so that you obviously cannot see the number the volunteer writes.

Then ask the volunteer to reverse the number and subtract the lower number from the higher number.

For example:

$$821$$
$$-128$$
$$693$$

Then reverse this number $$396$$
and add it to the answer $$1089$$
you just got

You can now announce to the group that the answer is 1089.

By the way, the answer will always be 1089.

Just a couple of minor rules: The original number must not be a mirror image of itself, such as 424. On occasion the initial subtraction will result in a two-digit number. For example:

$$786$$
$$-687$$
$$99$$

In such a case, simply ask the volunteer to add a zero in front of the two digits (change 99 to 099) and proceed.

Here's some more Hot Spice in the form of magic. In your calling around to the audio-visual suppliers, ask them if they have Retrophane.

Get your hands on a supply of this material and you will mystify your audience. Retrophane is a material used for transparencies that has special chemicals in it. Using a special marker, you can write directly on a blank piece of the material while it is projected on the screen. The surprise is that your writing or drawing will disappear after about six to eight seconds. You can then write or draw something else and it, too, will vanish after a few seconds.

Retrophane has great versatility when used for a regular finished

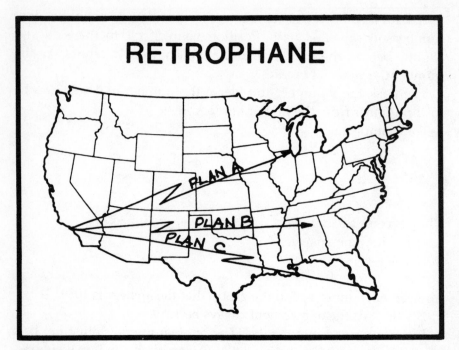

FIGURE 9L What you write on Retrophane will vanish before their eyes in six to eight seconds.

transparency. Figure 9L, for example, shows a map of the United States that has been copied onto Retrophane as a regular transparency. Communication lines from the home office to various branch locations can be drawn as as plan "A." Then in a few seconds as plan A vanishes, you can draw a different line for plan "B," then one for plan "C," and so on.

The next two optical illusions can precede the introduction of, "I have good news and bad news. Do you see the good news or the bad news?"

The first picture shows either a profile of a beautiful woman, or a witch. The second shows either a beautiful woman seated before a mirror, or a human skull.

Figure 9N shows an interesting technique. I have this projected on the screen several seconds before I get around to talking about it. I then announce that if you have this disease, you need to get out

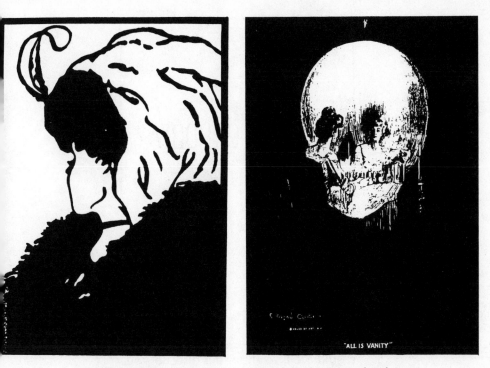

FIGURE 9M Hot Spice to introduce good news or bad news.

of here fast. Because this is the name of a morbid fear of money and that's what we are going to be talking about.

One technique of getting an audience to remember something is to use repetition. For example:

- Tell the audience
- Show a visual that illustrates the same thing
- Tell a joke or story that has the same message
- Give a demonstration of the same thing.

In Figure 9O is another way to use repetition with an element of surprise, in conjunction with the revelation technique.

In addition to the Hot Spice there are quickie items that we might

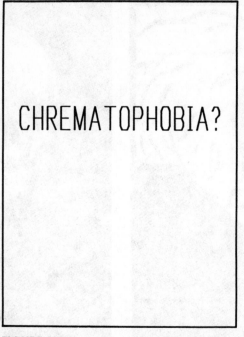

FIGURE 9N If you have this disease, you need to get out of here. That's a morbid fear of money.

call Salt and Pepper. These are nice to sprinkle throughout your presentation where they can be tied in to the subject.

Here are some samples of Salt and Pepper.

One way to use the following is to flash them on the screen to start the meeting. This is a technique that allows you to start the meeting on time, but still gives you a few minutes' delay for the people to assemble before you start your presentation.

EVERYONE WHO DOES NOT WORK HAS A SCHEME THAT DOES.

IF THERE ARE ONLY TWO PROGRAMS WORTH WATCHING, THEY WILL BOTH BE ON AT THE SAME TIME.

THE ONE THING THAT HOLDS THE WHOLE THING TOGETHER WILL BE MISSING.

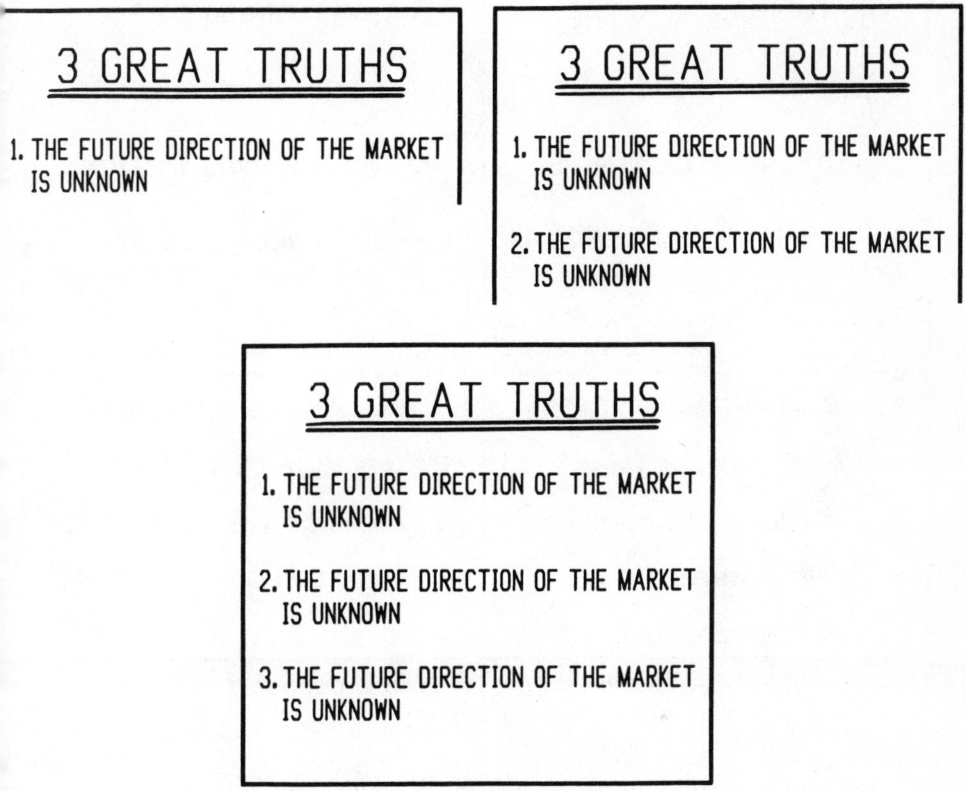

3 GREAT TRUTHS

1. THE FUTURE DIRECTION OF THE MARKET
   IS UNKNOWN

---

3 GREAT TRUTHS

1. THE FUTURE DIRECTION OF THE MARKET
   IS UNKNOWN

2. THE FUTURE DIRECTION OF THE MARKET
   IS UNKNOWN

---

3 GREAT TRUTHS

1. THE FUTURE DIRECTION OF THE MARKET
   IS UNKNOWN

2. THE FUTURE DIRECTION OF THE MARKET
   IS UNKNOWN

3. THE FUTURE DIRECTION OF THE MARKET
   IS UNKNOWN

FIGURE 90 The use of repetition, surprise, and the revelation technique.

YOU GET THE MOST OF WHAT YOU NEED THE LEAST.

THE OTHER LINE ALWAYS MOVES FASTER.

WHEN A POLITICIAN GETS AN IDEA, HE USUALLY GETS IT WRONG.

A SURPRISE MONETARY WINDFALL WILL BE ACCOMPANIED BY AN UNEXPENDED EXPENSE OF THE SAME AMOUNT.

YOU CAN ALWAYS FIND WHAT YOU'RE NOT LOOKING FOR.

THE MOST EXPENSIVE COMPONENT IS THE ONE THAT BREAKS.

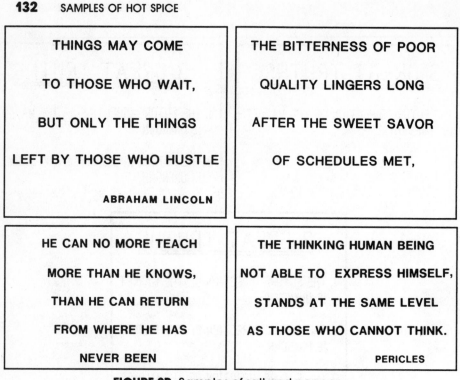

THINGS MAY COME

TO THOSE WHO WAIT,

BUT ONLY THE THINGS

LEFT BY THOSE WHO HUSTLE

ABRAHAM LINCOLN

THE BITTERNESS OF POOR

QUALITY LINGERS LONG

AFTER THE SWEET SAVOR

OF SCHEDULES MET,

HE CAN NO MORE TEACH

MORE THAN HE KNOWS,

THAN HE CAN RETURN

FROM WHERE HE HAS

NEVER BEEN

THE THINKING HUMAN BEING

NOT ABLE TO EXPRESS HIMSELF,

STANDS AT THE SAME LEVEL

AS THOSE WHO CANNOT THINK.

PERICLES

FIGURE 9P Samples of salt and pepper.

WHEN THE PLANE YOU'RE ON IS LATE, THE ONE YOU'RE CONNECTING TO IS ON TIME.

NO MATTER WHAT GOES WRONG, THERE IS ALWAYS SOMEBODY WHO KNEW IT WOULD.

NO TWO IDENTICAL PARTS ARE ALIKE.

WHEN THINGS ARE GOING WELL, SOMETHING WILL GO WRONG.

IF YOU DON'T NEED IT AND DON'T WANT IT, YOU CAN HAVE TONS OF IT.

YOU CAN ALWAYS HIT WHAT YOU DON'T AIM AT.

ANYONE WHO IS POPULAR IS BOUND TO BE DISLIKED.

LAST YEAR'S WAS ALWAYS BETTER.

IF YOU HAVE THE TIME, YOU WON'T HAVE THE MONEY.

THE MAN WHO WANTS

TO DO BUSINESS WITH YOU

CAN JUSTIFY ANYTHING

I KNOW YOU BELIEVE YOU

UNDERSTAND WHAT YOU THINK

I SAID, BUT I AM NOT SURE

YOU REALIZE THAT WHAT YOU

HEARD IS NOT WHAT I MEANT

FIGURE 9Q Samples of salt and pepper.

IF YOU HAVE THE MONEY, YOU WON'T HAVE THE TIME.

THE SHORTEST ROUTE HAS THE STEEPEST HILLS.

WHEN YOU TRY TO PROVE TO SOMEONE THAT A MACHINE WON'T WORK, IT WILL.

THE DIRECTION OF TAKE-OFF WILL BE OPPOSITE FROM THE DESTINATION.

1. HOW MANY ANIMALS OF EACH SPECIES DID MOSES TAKE ABOARD THE ARK WITH HIM DURING THE GREAT FLOOD?

   NONE...MOSES?

2. THE YANKEES AND THE TIGERS PLAY 5 BASEBALL GAMES. THEY EACH WIN 3 GAMES. THERE ARE NO TIES OR DISPUTED GAMES INVOLVED. HOW COME?

   WHO SAID THEY WERE PLAYING EACH OTHER?

3. ACCORDING TO INTERNATIONAL LAW, IF AN AIRPLANE SHOULD CRASH ON THE EXACT BORDER BETWEEN TWO COUNTRIES, WOULD THE UNIDENTIFIED SURVIVORS BE BURIED IN THE COUNTRY THEY WERE TRAVELING "TO" ... OR THE COUNTRY THEY WERE TRAVELING "FROM"?

   ...BURY SURVIVORS?

4. AN ARCHEOLOGIST CLAIMS HE HAS DUG UP A COIN THAT IS CLEARLY DATED 46 BC. HOW DO YOU KNOW THAT THE ARCHEOLOGIST IS NOT TELLING THE TRUTH?

   ...DATE A COIN "BC"?

5. A MAN BUILDS AN ORDINARY HOUSE WITH FOUR SIDES, EXCEPT THAT EACH SIDE HAS A SOUTHERN EXPOSURE. A BEAR COMES TO THE DOOR AND RINGS THE DOORBELL. WHAT COLOR IS THE BEAR?

   ...WHITE...POLAR BEAR ON NORTH POLE.

FIGURE 9R Samples of salt and pepper.

THERE IS NO JOB SO SIMPLE THAT IT CANNOT BE DONE WRONG.

THE DURATION OF THE MARRIAGE IS INVERSELY PROPORTIONAL TO THE COST OF THE WEDDING.

IF IT'S GOOD THEY DISCONTINUE IT.

THERE IS NO LIMIT TO HOW BAD THINGS CAN GET.

IF EVERYTHING IS COMING YOUR WAY, YOU'RE IN THE WRONG LANE.

CHAPTER 10

Questions, Answers, And Troublemakers

QUESTIONS

What would you guess is the single most important weapon to use in getting attention, keeping interest, and receiving feedback on how you're doing?

You just read the correct answer. It's the question. Nothing can do so much for so many as the question. And nothing is as effective as the question to give you immediate feedback on the comprehension, understanding, and agreement of the audience. Questions are an essential and integral part of an effective presentation. Not just any question, but well-thought-out, preplanned and prepositioned questions. And the planned question is an important item on your cheat sheet.

You should consider a question for either the introduction of a key point or as a way of finalizing the key point, or both.

For example, in presenting my company's corporate strategy, I introduce a key point by asking the audience whether they think our company is primarily a technology-driven company or primarily a market-driven company. Well, let me tell you, that really gets the juices flowing. Most people had never thought about the company in those terms. Not only do they voluntarily start responding, they start arguing with each other. Nobody ever went to sleep during that question, or the presentation of the material that followed on that subject.

The key to the question is to make it stimulating and thought provoking: questions that call on experience, views, or opinions. Questions that start with phrases like, "What is your opinion of . . .?" or, "What is the first thing you would do if . . .?" or, "What do you think is the cause of . . .?"

What we do *not* want are mundane questions with a self-evident answer of yes or no.

You do want to cause early success with the audience, so you'll want the first few questions to be easy to answer.

The most dramatic and tongue-in-cheek example of causing early success I ever saw was a presenter who asked a member of the audience to pick a number between 1 and 10. He responded with "four." The presenter said, "That's the correct answer." Of course, any answer would have been the correct answer.

On a more serious note, you should ask questions that:

- Relate to the key point you are presenting
- Are clear and concise
- Emphasize one point only
- Reveal the audience's understanding

There are different types of questions and different questioning techniques. Here are some types of questions that are suited for an audience size of fewer than 50 people.

The Rifle Shot Question

This is where you make eye contact with a specific individual, call him by name, then ask the question. This is the most common type of question.

The Time Bomb Question

This is where you ask the question of the audience as a group, then call on a specific person to answer only after you have finished the question. This is an effective technique for getting attention and keeping interest. After a few of these types of questions, the audience will really perk up since they don't know who is going to be called on to answer—and nobody wants to be embarrassed by not knowing what the question was.

The Ricochet Question

This is where you redirect a question that has been asked of you to another member of the audience. This is a good technique if you want a little more time to think about your answer. It is also helpful in assessing the understanding of the audience about the subject. It's effective for audience participation and especially good for handling some types of troublemakers, as we shall see shortly.

The Rebound Question

This is where the presenter rephrases the question and directs it back to the person who asked it. This technique is also good for certain types of troublemakers and tends to reduce or eliminate frivolous questions.

Which type of question is the best?

No single one, but *all* of the above. It is best to have a mix of questions, with the inherent elements of suspense and surprise.

These types of questioning techniques presuppose that you either know the people or they have tent cards to facilitate calling them by name. But what if you don't know the people, and they don't have tent cards? The answer is a seating chart. A seating chart is an 8½ × 11 piece of paper with the names of the people and their relative position in the room.

The simplest and easiest way to get a seating chart is to ask the host or person running the meeting if they have one. Sometimes, but not often, they will.

The next best way is to sit in on the meeting kick-off if the attendees are asked to introduce themselves. Have the room arrangement roughed out with the boxes for each position. Then all you have to do is write their names in the boxes. This has the added advantage that you can also make brief notes about special backgrounds, experiences, skills, and so forth. This will allow you to personalize and tailor your questions to specific individuals.

Another way of getting a seating chart with names is to sit in the back of the room and ask a staff member, or another presenter who is familiar with the audience, to help you fill in the names.

If none of the above works you can still sit in on other presentations and listen to names as they are used by other presenters, or by attendees among themselves before the meeting and at coffee breaks. Using this technique, you can get at least 25 percent of the names. That's all you need to personalize your questions.

In any event, get some names. You want to direct your question to John by name, not by, "Hey you."

Well, all that Q and A is fine for a small audience, but what if it's a larger group? You can't really have questions and answers for a large group, right? Wrong. You sure can have questions for a large group—you just change your style and use a different technique.

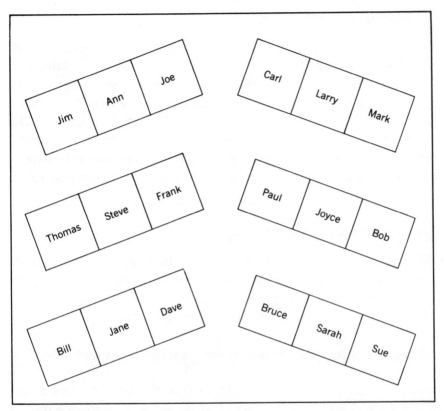

FIGURE 10A A seating chart will allow us to call on people by name.

The key is to phrase the question in such a way that it causes a short answer and provides a hint to the type of answer we are looking for.

For example, we have the sing-a-long.

The Sing-Along Question

Here the question is directed not to an individual, but to the entire audience. Examples: "The bottom line reason we're in business is to make_____" (What?). Or, if I were talking about the relationship between unit cost and volume, I might say, "If I increase the volume the unit cost will go_____" (Which way?).

Another version of the sing-along question is to ask for a show of hands on a subject, an opinion, an experience, and so on.

The Multiple Choice Question

Here we give the audience a hint by suggesting some answers. For example, in talking about lawyers I make the following statement: "You would probably guess that we have more lawyers per 1000 of population than the Japanese. . . . But how many more? . . . Twice as many? . . . Three times as many? . . . Ten times as many?" The key to this technique is to make brief eye contact with multiple people as you call out the multiple choices. At the same time extend your arm in a gesture of directing the question to multiple people.

The Ask and Answer Question

This is a technique where you ask a question, pause, and then answer it yourself. For example, "Of all the stockbrokers in the country, what percent would you guess don't own any stock?" (Pause) "Would you believe 70 percent of all stockbrokers don't own any stock?"

Please, let's not use the mundane "Are there any questions?" If we have done our homework, we will have planned provocative questions that will be of interest to the audience. Answers to the questions will let you know whether or not your audience understands and agrees.

Don't let your mind trick you into false thinking about the value and importance of questions. For example:

- They're more trouble than they're worth.

  Answer: Not true. It's not a lot of trouble. It is a lot of planning. As for its value—there is no known substitute.

- I just don't have the time. There's too much material to cover.

  Answer: You do have the time. You will do much better to cover less material with questions and discussion than more material without.

- I'm afraid I'll lose control.

  Answer: Not if you do your homework and plan the content

and position of each question. What we're looking for is a controlled discussion using questions.

- I'm afraid I'll get into arguments and personality conflicts with loudmouth know-it-alls.

  Answer: Not if you follow the rules of how to handle the troublemaker.

- I'm more comfortable just giving a straight presentation.

  Answer: You may be. However, the primary objective of your presentation says nothing about your comfort level. You are more likely to achieve your objective if you have interaction with the audience.

There is no better way to get attention and keep interest than a well-thought-out and well-planned question. It is natural for people to want to know the answer to a good question. Questions will also enhance the comprehension and retention of the material.

Questions are just as important to you the presenter. The quality of the answers let you know how effectively you are communicating your message. Areas of misunderstanding are quickly identified.

If the answers to questions in a particular area are consistently vague, or wide off the mark, then you need to either spend more time in that area or, more likely, think of a different conceptual way of presenting the information—such as using an analogy.

Here is something you will run into when giving a presentation to different levels of people within the same organization. People at the bottom of the organizational chart are sometimes reluctant to express an opinion until they know which way the wind is blowing at the top of the organization. So direct a few early questions to the top of the mountain. Make sure they are opinion questions. There are no wrong answers to an opinion question. That will clear the air for the rest of the climbers. Even better is to get the top man to introduce you and the subject and announce his support and endorsement. That guarantees a successful presentation.

ANSWERS

So far we have talked only about questions you would ask of the audience. But what about the other side of the coin? How do we handle questions that are asked of us?

The first thing you must do is create a penalty-free environment for asking questions. The audience must know that it is safe to ask a question. That there will be no ridicule, no rudeness, and no sarcasm. Never say or do anything that will make the questioner feel stupid or foolish. If in fact they are, let the audience come to that conclusion—not you.

In creating an open and positive environment for questions, our body language speaks louder than our words. For example, if you say, "Are there any questions?" while looking at your notes or down at the floor, your body language says, "I'm not interested in your questions."

If you genuinely want questions it will be evident to the audience. If you don't, it will be just as evident.

To a large degree you can control the number of questions and the content of the questions. Here's how. At the end of a presentation, when you have some quiet time to yourself, flip back through your cheat sheets and make a note of what questions were asked and where. After you have given the presentation a few times, consistent patterns of questions will begin to develop. It's a simple matter then to incorporate the answers into your presentation. That way, those questions will never be asked.

On the other hand, you might plan on not answering some specific common questions. Then, when the question is asked, you appear to be giving a spontaneous answer. But it is actually a carefully rehearsed response. This is a particularly impressive technique if the answer involves statistics, dates, names, places, and so on, which you have rehearsed and noted on your cheat sheet.

Now to some Do's and Don'ts on answering questions.

Listen to the Question

Carefully. Have you ever been in a meeting where someone asks a question and half way through the question the presenter interrupts the questioner and says, "The answer is so-and-so"? Then the questioner replies, "That was not my question."

What happened here is that the presenter assumed that this question was going to be the same as other questions that had been asked before.

Do not make that mistake. Do not interrupt. Even if you are correct about what the question is, the other members of the audience want and need to hear the complete question.

Repeat the Question

If you don't the audience will ask, "What was the question?" If they don't ask it, they will be thinking it. This problem is most common when the question comes from the front of the room. Typically, those in the back of the room can't hear the questions from the front of the room.

In my company when we get a new instructor on board, an experienced instructor will sit in the back of the room for their first few presentations. The experienced instructor will have three pre-printed signs which can be held up as a flag to the new presenter. They say:

"Louder"

"5 Minutes"

"Repeat the Question"

(That tells you the three most common problems with our presenters.)

You want to do more than simply repeat the question. You want to rephrase the question and direct your answer, not to the person who asked it, but to the entire audience. This will enhance the interest of the entire audience in the subject and your answer.

There is a side benefit in this technique. It gives you more thinking time to formulate your answer. We talk slow but the brain is fast. When we rephrase and repeat the question there are a lot of surplus nanoseconds for the brain to organize its answer. So give yourself that extra time. You'll have a better answer.

Eye Contact

Look directly at the person while the question is being asked, but when you answer, break eye contact with that person and direct your attention to the entire audience.

Answering Mistakes

The three most common mistakes in answering questions are:

1. Answering too much. Keep your answers brief and to the point. If you answer a question with a speech, you sure put a damper on other questions being asked.

   Long-winded answers are boring, do not help your case, and will cause the audience to tune out.

2. Answering too soon. This is the interrupt problem we talked about that causes you to answer the wrong question.

3. Dialogue with one person. Don't allow yourself to fall into a dialogue with one person. Offer to speak with the individual at the end of the program, break eye contact, and move on.

Don't Bluff

If you don't know the answer or aren't sure—don't bluff. And don't hesitate, either. If you do, your body language says, "I'm not sure of this answer, but I'm going to try it." Instead be prompt to admit that you do not know the answer. If it's important to the subject at hand then volunteer to find out. Make a written note to yourself (that's important). One effective technique is to reserve a page of a flip chart for questions you are going to follow up. That demonstrates interest and sincerity to the audience.

Don't be embarrassed or apologetic about not having all the answers. If you did, you wouldn't be where you are, and you wouldn't be doing what you're doing.

Don't Insult the Questioner

You will if you say, "Your question isn't clear." A better way is ask the person to repeat the question.

TROUBLEMAKERS

Let's Talk about Troublemakers

The first thing we need to realize is that out of every 100 people, there's at least one nut. We need to recognize that we simply are not going to convert a hostile attitude about our company, our product, our service, or a new idea in a one-hour presentation. What we can hope to do is to neutralize the participation and the effect of the hostile troublemaker.

Further, even among fair-minded people, not everyone will want to sing word for word out of our songbook. It's important for us to have a realistic attitude about our audience and our expectations. If we anticipate the troublemaker, we are less likely to come unglued when someone says, "It'll never work." The best way to anticipate the audience is to take the time to get background information on the audience. This will allow you to better understand the opinions, feelings, and biases of those who are likely to disagree with you.

If on the basis of your homework you anticipate disagreement, or if the nature of your subject is somewhat controversial and likely to arouse strong feelings, you should address the disagreement before it addresses you. The best way to ward off trouble is to head it off at the pass. The way we do that is to recognize in our early remarks that there are some other points of view on this subject. Then—and this is important—you state in summary form the other point of view. If you are the one who brings it up, you can explain it in your words and within the context of the view you are going to present. That will burst the balloon of the hostile troublemaker. You have stated his case for him and thereby taken the sting out of his comments. The audience will appreciate the fairness and evenhandedness of recognizing other points of view. The bottom line effect of this is to lend credibility and strength to your case.

We will now categorize the troublemakers and talk further about techniques of neutralizing, defusing, and minimizing their effect.

The Hostile Troublemaker

He is the worst of all. He or she is the one who'll burst out with statements like, "That'll never happen"; "It'll never work"; "I don't agree." His remarks may even take the form of a personal attack on you or what you represent.

One strategy for handling the hostile troublemaker is to persuade the rest of the audience to your way of thinking before the troublemaker can do his damage. The way we do this is to preface our presentation with a remark like the following: "For the next 30 minutes I am going to present a new concept. I would like to ask that we just have an open mind and hold our comments or questions until I finish. Is that all right?" Of course the group will agree that it's all right. Then if the troublemaker tries to interrupt we can merely reference the agreement of the group to hold comments until we finish the presentation of the new concept. If you have followed the Blueprint for Success you will have persuaded the audience to your view. If the troublemaker now makes a statement like, "It'll never work," he will tend to be put down by the audience and viewed as not having an open mind. And rather than you responding to the troublemaker's comment, it's more effective if you let another member of the audience respond. Now his or her disagreement is not with you, but with the rest of the audience. That's like a hammer to the head. The message to the troublemaker is, "Shut up."

Another way of defusing the troublemaker is to use the weight-of-evidence technique. Since you know what you are going to present, you will also know the more common objections. That being the case, you can prepare yourself in advance with facts, figures, references, quotes, and so forth for the common objections. The strategy is to drown the troublemaker with the weight of the evidence you have prepared or collected. He is disadvantaged since he is not as prepared as you are for an intelligent discussion. Your dialogue might sound like this: "You may be right, but let me review the facts and the evidence that supports my position." You can now, once again, turn to the audience for support.

Hostile questions sometimes have hostile words imbedded in the question. Words like rip-off, sneaky, hedging. You can defuse these words by asking for clarification. Do not repeat hostile words when you rephrase the questions. In fact, a truly hostile question that is loaded with emotion should not be repeated. Approach it instead as follows: "I can't answer your entire question. If, however, what you mean by _____ is _____ then my answer is _____." Or, "If what you would like to know is _____, then my answer is _____." Clearly state your position but do not let the interrogator goad you into a debate or an emotional argument. Again, it's far better to ask for input from someone in the audience whom you know does not agree with the opinion of the troublemaker.

Another way of handling troublemakers is to let them destroy themselves. You do this by answering a hostile question with a question. "If you feel that way about the situation, then what do you think should be done to correct it?" The answers to these kinds of questions tend to be recognized by the audience as more emotional than well-thought-out, logical answers. The longer he talks the more the troublemaker hurts himself. It starts to become apparent that he has an ax to grind.

Negative comments or questions are not always hostile. Some people just like to argue or play the devil's advocate. You know the type. You say it's hot, they say it's cold. Their comments or questions tend to be nit-picking, directing attention away from your central point. The strategy here is to get their agreement on the larger point. You can then respond with, "Although we have a difference on the detail, we're in agreement on the concept."

Finally, don't lose your cool. Avoid eye contact with the troublemaker. The more visual contact you have with the troublemaker, the more irritated you will become. If all else fails, just say, "It looks like we have different views on this subject. Why don't we discuss it in more detail after the meeting?" Strange thing. Rarely do they want to discuss the subject after the meeting. They seem to be more interested in a verbal interchange in front of an audience. Guess that tells us something about the troublemaker.

The Know-It-All Troublemaker

This one has a club used to intimidate people. Some types of clubs are:

- Length of service
- Advanced degree
- Experience
- Title
- Professional status

Their remarks are prefaced with:

- "I have a Ph.D. in Economics and. . . ."
- "I have worked on this project more than anyone in the room and. . . ."
- "In my 20 years of experience. . . ."
- "As a senior systems analyst my opinion is. . . ."

The unstated assumption here is that he knows more than you do, hence he is right and you are wrong.

The key to handling the know-it-all is to stick to the facts. Do not theorize or speculate. Stick to your own experiences and well-documented evidence. People can legitimately question and disagree with your theory or your speculation. But they cannot question your experience or documented facts.

Another way of handling the know-it-all troublemaker is to use quotes of other experts whose credentials are even greater than those of the troublemaker.

Let me tell you another approach I stumbled on by accident. Often you know in advance or can find out in advance if you are going to have any know-it-alls in the audience. Arrange a meeting with them in advance. Acknowledge their credentials. Tell them what you are going to present and ask for their support. You will be amazed more often than not to find that they will support and endorse your program. So what started out to be a problem has now become a reference.

Let's take the worst case scenario. Suppose the know-it-all will not support you. You can still take the sting out of his punch by announcing in advance that you and he do not agree and here's why. You are stating his case for him and thereby defusing him.

The Loudmouth Troublemaker

This is the person who talks too much, too loud, dominates the meeting, and seems impossible to shut up.

The most subtle techniques for coping with loudmouths involve your physical position in relation to them. Try moving closer and closer to them while they are talking and maintain eye contact until you are standing right in front of them. Your physical presence—you are standing, they are sitting—will often make them aware of their behavior and they will stop talking.

Here are some other techniques for dealing with loudmouths:

- Interrupt them with the question, "What would you say is your main point?"
- Make eye contact with the loudmouth and say, "I appreciate your comments, but we would like to also hear from other people."
- After a reasonable amount of time ask the loudmouth, "What is your question?"
- Questions that are vague, open-ended, or not relevant can be answered as follows:
  - "I'm not qualified to give you an intelligent answer to that question."
  - "That's a good question, but in the short time we have I would like to stick to the subject of _____."
  - "Interesting point, but how does it relate to the subject of _____?"
- Avoid eye contact and conveniently don't see their hands.
- Ask them to record, take notes, or list questions and "to-do's" for follow-up. (That will keep them busy.)
- Finally, during a coffee break you can recognize their interest in

the subject, but tell them you are running behind because of the open discussion, and ask for their support in keeping the discussion down. You could even suggest they jot down questions they would like to discuss with you after the meeting.

The Interrupter Troublemaker

This type starts talking before others are finished. Often, the interrupter doesn't mean to be rude, but becomes impatient and overly excited. Like the loudmouth, the interrupter is afraid that a new, red-hot idea will be lost if it isn't blurted out immediately.

There is a simple and easy solution to the interrupter. Every time they start doing it, jump in and say, "Wait a minute Jim, let's let John finish what he was saying." After you do this a few times the interrupter will get the message.

The Interpreter Troublemaker

They continually want to speak for other people. They can always be recognized by the phrase "What John is really trying to say is . . . ," or "What I hear John saying is. . . ."

The first part of our solution is the same as for the interrupter. If John is still in the middle of talking we want to jump in quickly and say, "Wait a minute, let's let John speak for himself. Go ahead, John, finish what you were saying."

If John has already finished talking, then turn to him and ask, "John, do you think Jim correctly understood what you said? Was his restatement an accurate representation of what you were saying?"

A couple of these will cure the interpreter real quick.

The Gossiper Troublemakers

They introduce gossip, rumors, and hearsay into the discussion. Valuable time can be wasted arguing over whether something is true or not.

"Isn't there a regulation that you can't . . . ?"

"It seems like I remember that. . . ."

"I thought I heard so and so say. . . ."

Immediately ask if anyone can confirm or verify the accuracy of the statement. If they cannot, then give the ball back to the gossiper with the statement, "Let's not take the time of the audience until we can verify the accuracy of the information."

The Whisperer Troublemaker

Nothing is more irritating to a presenter than two people whispering while you are presenting. There are two solutions.

One is to walk up close to the whisperers and make eye contact with them. The other is to stop talking and establish dead silence. When you do, what was a whisper becomes a roar—and an embarrassment to the whisperers.

The Silent Troublemaker

They sit in the back of the room, don't say anything, may be reading a newspaper, rolling their eyes, shaking their heads, crossing and uncrossing legs, pushing their chair back from the table, and so forth. In many ways they are the most difficult of all. At least with the overtalkative participants, you know where you stand. With the silent treatment, you don't know if they understand what you're talking about, aren't interested, are thinking about something else, are shy and unassertive, aren't interested in the subject, don't like you, or what.

The only real weapon you have for silent troublemakers is the Rifleshot Question. Call them by name, then follow with an open question that calls for an opinion, an experience, an example, and so on.

The other thing you can do is talk to them at the break on a personal basis about the subject, their understanding, their questions, their agreement or disagreement, or what have you.

In presentations, as in life, the silent treatment can be the worst. And as in life, there are no magic answers, just a need for patience and tolerance.

The Busy-Busy Troublemakers

They are always ducking in and out of the meeting, constantly receiving messages or rushing out to take a phone call, or deal with a crisis. What's worse, the busy-busy is often the manager or senior person in the meeting. That's why he or she feels so free to come and go. But by doing so, the busy-busy ends up wasting his or her time, and the time of the rest of the participants. During each departure, the meeting may come to a standstill. Or the busy-busy has to be briefed upon reentry. Often there is no point in continuing a meeting if a key person is absent.

There are four ways of dealing with the busy-busy troublemaker.

1. The simplest and most effective way is to hold the presentation on your turf or neutral turf, and not his home ground. That way you remove him from his support systems, and you will be in control of the messages.

2. Another solution is to schedule the presentation either before or after normal business hours.

3. If you have to give the presentation on his turf, then you can announce in advance the time and duration of the break for coffee and phone calls. He will usually get the message.

4. Sometimes you will know in advance that you will have this problem because you know the individual. If that's the case then go to Mr. or Ms. Busy-Busy and tell him or her that you want to schedule the presentation on a date and time they will be able to attend with minimum interruption. Again, they will usually get the message.

The Latecomer Troublemaker

This is a tough one, but here are some thoughts:

- Pick an odd time for the meeting or presentation to start. Don't pick 8:30 or 9:00. Have it announced and publicized that the presentation will start at 8:47. That kind of a start time is a tip-off to the attendees that this meeting is probably really going to start at 8:47.

- You can also have it announced and publicized that a door prize will be awarded at 8:48. The value of the door prize is not important. It can even be a novelty item.

- Make remarks to the latecomer only if it feels natural and comfortable for your body chemistry. And smile when you make them, such as

  "I'm sorry, I must have started early."

  "Are you the one who's giving the lecture on time management?"

- Stop talking and establish dead silence while the latecomer makes his way to a seat.

- Establish a late kitty. Anyone late for a meeting has to put a quarter or a dollar in the late kitty (used for coffee and rolls).

- Announce to the latecomer that she has been volunteered to do some follow-up staff work.

The Early-Leaver Troublemaker

Few things are more disconcerting to a presenter than someone standing up and walking out in the middle of the presentation.

The best way to stop this is to get the audience to agree in advance that it will not happen. You can do this by announcing the time that the presentation will be over, and then asking if anyone has a problem with that schedule. If no one says anything, then we have established a gentlemen's agreement. A potential early-leaver would be pretty embarrassed to walk out after that.

If anyone does state they cannot stay for the entire presentation, he or she will usually volunteer a legitimate reason.

CHAPTER 11

Bad habits, mannerisms, and other distractions can literally *destroy* a presentation that has a good opening, a powerful close, is well organized, has excellent visual aids, lots of hot spice, and is delivered with enthusiasm.

As we get into specifics you are going to think, "That's really nit-picking," but a presentation is the sum of a thousand nits. And just as a drop of dye can turn an entire glass of water murky, so, too, can a single distracting mannerism turn a good presentation very sour very fast. Once you've turned them off, you'll never get them back. If the guys in the back row have money on the table and are keeping score on the number of "ah's," "uh's," or ear lobe pulls, then you have lost the game. Non-verbal communications is strong medicine. What we *do* can speak much louder than what we *say*. For example: If you stand up in front of an audience with a frown on your face, look down at the floor, and say, "I'm really excited to be here," the immediate interpretation is—"You lie." Or, if you unbutton your jacket, and place both hands on your hips like a cowboy ready for a shoot-out and announce, "Y'all feel free to ask any questions at any time"—the real message to the audience is, "Don't you dare ask any questions." Your body language and your voice can reinforce your words or destroy your message. Your visual and auditory clues tell the audience more clearly how you feel about the subject than do your words. A presenter who talks in a monotone, has a frozen stance, and an absence of enthusiasm, is saying, "Take it or leave it."

Let's talk about some of the components of body language and voice.

POSTURE

Some distracting characteristics are:

- Slouching
- Speaking with head bowed
- Hanging on to supports for dear life: lectern, flip-chart stand, table, and so on
- Rigid—like a military position

- Rocking from side to side or
- Rocking front to back—heel to toe

Sometimes there are posture characteristics that seem to go with certain jobs.

One time I was down in Florida making a presentation to a conference on "How to Give an Effective Presentation." I was speaking to the point of posture characteristics that seem to go with certain jobs, and I used the example of branch managers in my company. I demonstrated the most common characteristics of our branch managers—which is to unbutton the jacket, put both hands in the pants pockets, and bounce up and down on the balls of the feet.

Well, the next morning was the wrap-up of the conference. Unknown to me, the final speaker was a big, *big* shot from my company. This was a really big deal. With 500 people in the audience he walks out on the stage, unbuttons his jacket, puts both hands in his pants pockets, and says, "Good morning, ladies and gentlemen" while bouncing up and down on the balls of his feet. Well, this broke the audience up. Of course, he didn't know what was going on. As the audience was laughing you could see stark terror on his face as he looked down to see if his fly was unzipped. Well, that really broke the audience up. Afterward somebody told him what had happened. He sent me to Europe. Took me two years to get back.

SMOKING AND DRINKING

I know you've been in meetings where the presenter was sipping coffee and/or smoking a cigarette while trying to present.

Let me just make a flat statement on that subject. *Don't do it.* Not only is it distracting—it's bad manners.

FACIAL EXPRESSION

If you walk down the street and just look at the expressions on people's faces, you rarely see a smile. Mostly you see a deadpan or severe look—sometimes a scowling or an apathetic expression.

You don't want to be caught in front of an audience looking like that. What's the answer? The answer is to smile. But most of us forget to smile. The solution is to write the word "SMILE" in red on about every fourth cheat sheet. Just looking at the word will cause you to smile.

GUARANTEED DISTRACTIONS

Here are some bad habits that are guaranteed to take the mind of the audience off the subject. These are like drops of dirty dye in the clear water of your presentation.

- Rattling keys or coins in your pocket
- The habitual and continuing use of "uhs" or "ahs." Some people double-clutch it and say "uh-uh" or "ah-ah."
- Sucking the teeth
- Ring twisting
- Stroking a beard
- Lip licking
- Tugging your ear
- Lip biting
- Cracking knuckles
- Pushing the bridge of your glasses
- Playing with a watch
- Drumming your finger
- Bouncing a pencil on its eraser
- Blowing hair out of your eyes
- Popping the top of a Magic Marker
- Extending and retracting a telescoping pointer

Some are exclusive to females:

- Twirling hair
- Playing with beads, gold chains, or other jewelry

Let me ask you a question. If you had any of these bad habits, do you think you would be aware of them? Probably not. For example, I know a lady who did a lot of presentations on a particular subject. She was excellent. No one had more experience or knew the subject better. There was just one problem. She had a bad habit. She used a flip chart in her presentation, so she always had a Magic Marker in her hand. Her bad habit was the popping of the top of the Magic Marker about every 10 seconds.

Well, the popping of the top of a Magic Marker doesn't make a very loud noise, but if you're doing it every 10 seconds that's six times a minute, or 360 times an hour. By the time you get up to pop number 125, they start to sound like rifle shots.

Do you think she was aware of what she was doing? Did she hear the noise? Absolutely not. But to the audience that sound became magnified 20-fold. And, ironically, your best friends will rarely tell you. One of the reasons is that they have not only learned to put up with these habits, they have also learned to tune them out. What to do? Coming shortly.

EYE CONTACT

This is a way for you to say to every person in the audience, "You are important. I'm talking just to you."

And yet, too often the presenter will focus on the floor or the ceiling, tend to look at the same two or three people, or stare over the heads of the audience. Sometimes the presenter will have a visual obsession with one side of the room to the exclusion of the other.

Lack of eye contact gives the impression that you are talking at people instead of to people.

There is another important reason for eye contact. It is the source of feedback that tells you how you're doing. Are they with you? Do they understand? Do they agree? Are you moving too fast? Are you belaboring a point? You will never know if you don't look at them.

For small groups you can have eye contact with every person multiple times. But it doesn't happen automatically. It requires a conscious and planned effort on your part. For a large audience you can create the illusion of individual contact by focusing on a few specific people in various parts of the room. Focus on one, then sweep your eyes slowly to the next one. Don't throw darting glances. And don't forget the people on the extreme right and left or those in the last three rows.

MOVEMENT

What can be worse than a presenter who is frozen in one spot?

Answer: One who runs back and forth across the front of the room like a caged animal. We want and need movement, but it needs to be planned, deliberate, and controlled—not that of a lion in a cage.

GESTURES

Gestures are like movement. The only thing worse than none is too many. And as with movement, gestures should be smooth, deliberate, and natural. The purpose of gestures is to accent and reinforce your message. Please don't look like Robinson Crusoe waving at a passing plane.

DRESS

Entire books are written on this subject, but everything we need to know can be summarized in 10 seconds with two points:

1. People are most comfortable with people who are most like themselves. Clothes that are not appropriate for a particular group create an unnecessary obstacle for the presenter.

2. Don't dress for this job. Dress for your next job. Whatever job or position you aspire to, dress like the person who has that job or that position.

And get a haircut—increase your odds of success by 24 percent.

VOICE

The dominant source of *input* to human beings is visual. You would think the dominant source of *output* would be the spoken word. It is, but that's not the whole truth. *How* you say something can be more dominant than *what* you say.

Have you ever had a spat with the spouse, not over what was said but because of the manner or tone in which it was spoken? Just as we read between the lines we also listen between the words—not for *what* was said, but for *how* it was said.

For example, you can say the same words and convey three different messages:

- I really believe in what I'm saying.
- I don't have a lot of knowledge or experience on this subject.
- I don't care what you think, I'm just doing my job.

Some of the problems with the voice are:

- Monotone
- High pitch
- Volume drop at end of sentences
- Inaudibility
- Lack of variety in pace or volume
- Nasal sound
- Mumbling

These all fall under one or more of the four characteristics of the human voice: pitch, loudness, rate, and quality.

Pitch What we want to avoid is the monotony of the same pitch. What we want are variations or inflections.

Loudness Speaking too loudly is almost as bad as speaking too softly. You will have just the right volume if you imagine that you are talking to the people seated near the rear of the room. But remember, we need variations in loudness. Dropping the voice to a near whisper can be as effective for emphasis as raising it to a near shout. Some of both will do the job. Avoid the monotony of unvarying sound. It's wearing on the listener.

Rate Speaking too fast for too long inhibits effective communication. On the other hand, if you talk too slowly you will put people to sleep. The magic words are *variety, change* of *pace*, and *pause*. Failure to use the pause is one of the more common mistakes of presenters.

The master of pace and pause is the news commentator Paul Harvey. Rapid-fire words followed by a pause followed by a few seconds of slow pace is his effective technique. If you calculated the number of words per minute he speaks, they would be about the average of most speakers. But what a difference the peaks, valleys, and pauses make in the attentiveness of the audience. The right formula is fast, pause, slow.

Quality There are great differences in the quality of the voice of singers and of speakers. The quality of your voice is directly affected by your knowledge, confidence, and belief in the subject.

If you suspect that you might have a problem with the quality of your voice, you will find the answer in the chapter Rehearse, Rehearse, Rehearse—Then Cheat.

Words, Phrases, and Pronunciation A kissin' cousin to problems of voice characteristics is the use of certain words and phrases that detract from the effectiveness of presentations. We have already mentioned the "um's" and the "uh's," but there are others like:

- "Y'know"
- "Okay, okay"
- "Kind of"
- "Sort of"
- "Wonderful, wonderful"
- "You know what I mean?"

If you're not sure how to pronounce a word, either don't use it, or look it up. Pronunciation errors are often perceived by the listener as an indication of ignorance and poor preparation. Some people will automatically put you in the uneducated category if you use a word like "irregardless." What would they think if you said something like, "Git your camera out and take a pitcher of the athelete."

As we said, if you have some bad habits and distractions, you may be the last to know. Your best friend won't tell you. They have learned that there are few things in life more unwanted than unsolicited advice. So how are you going to find out?

The best way of all is to see yourself the way other people see you. That means videotape. If you ever have the opportunity to have yourself videotaped, don't pass it up. There is absolutely nothing as effective in dramatically hammering home your distracting habits as a videotape. It can be a humbling but invaluable experience—so brace yourself. On the other hand, if your name is Clarence Darrow or William Jennings Bryan, you can sit back and see how great you really are.

If you don't have access to a videotape machine, there are two other things you can do.

Borrow a cassette tape recorder and capture the vocal part of the presentation. This will let you hear what the audience hears. If you speak in a monotone with no change of pace or pitch, it will be immediately obvious.

The next thing you can do is to have a friend or colleague sit in the back as an observer, and critique you. Pick this person carefully.

He or she should be someone whose judgment you respect and whom you believe will be objective and candid. Your spouse is not a good candidate. Give them a critique sheet to follow. (See Getting Good, Getting Better—The Critique.) Ask them to note your strengths as well as your weaknesses. We are interested in improving our style, not destroying our confidence.

MISCELLANEOUS BUT IMPORTANT DISTRACTIONS

These distractions are listed last, but they can blow you out of the water as fast as anything else.

Misspelled Words

This is a no-no. People will think that if you're sloppy with your spelling, then you'll also be sloppy with your service or support.

Talking to the Board

Do not talk to the screen, board, or flip charts. Watch the weather man on T.V. Note how he describes the weather without talking to the screen.

Off-Center Projection

Now here is a real nit, but believe me, it can really irritate an audience. A simple little thing like centering the picture on the screen. Strange things can preoccupy the mind and this is one of them.

Out of Focus Projector

The first thing to do on entering the room is to check out the projector. The problem is the same as above. Little things can cause big problems.

External Noises

You are just asking for trouble if your meeting room is near the kitchen or the door to the kitchen. And who is meeting in the room next door? What if they have a jazz band for entertainment? Is the separation between rooms a solid wall or an accordion divider? If the meeting is at an airport hotel, guess what kind of noise you're going to be hearing? And don't wait until the day of the meeting to find out that your competitor is in the room next to yours.

External View

You might have a beautiful room, but what if it has picture windows overlooking the swimming pool? Worse, yet, what if they're having a fashion show on the deck of the pool or the swim suit contest for the local beauty queen. Don't think it can't happen to you.

CHAPTER 12

TIP #1   The Rule of 60 Percent

Only 60 percent will show up. So set up chairs for only 60 percent of the number you think will come. Keep some extra chairs nearby but out of sight.

When the 60 percent show up it will look like a packed house. If more show up, you can easily get the extra chairs for what is obviously an overflow crowd. Whatever happens, you have a full house. That's heads you win, tails you win.

But before you count your winnings, check out Tip #2.

TIP #2   Don't Be Alone in This Wicked World

That's what the people will feel like if you have a meeting for 10 in a room designed for 50. The room size is very important. It must be appropriate to the size of the group. Not too big, not too small, but just right.

TIP #3   You Can Be Special

There's no rule that says you have to provide a handout at the end. But you will be special if you do. People like getting something extra and free. Just a one-page summary will do the trick. Even better would be reprints of articles, a list of resources or numbers to call, a bibliography and a roster of attendees. Be sure to include your card, and your network will grow and grow.

TIP #4   If It Ain't Right, It Ain't Right

If someone's name gets misspelled on their badge or place card they will say it's okay—it's no big deal—it happens all the time. *Don't you believe it*. It's not okay and it is a big deal, so fix it now—right now. Have some blank badges and place cards ready and waiting.

TIP #5   Always Start and End with the Lights Full Bright

The opening and the close are the most important parts of the presentation. Be sure all projectors are off and the lights full bright so the focus is on you for the opening and the close.

TIP #6   If in Doubt—Don't

If you can make yourself heard without a microphone, don't use it. It seems like there is no limit to the things that can go wrong with a mike and a sound system. Often if a mike is available, a presenter will feel compelled to use it. Resist that feeling. If in doubt, do without.

TIP #7   How To Minimize the Mumbling, Whispering, and Cliques

You can control the seating by preprinting and positioning the place cards or tent cards in advance. Separate the folks who work together or play together. And position the females between two males. Both will like it better. And, I guarantee you, there will be less talking.

TIP #8   The Pendulum Is Over Here

Times are a-changing. Think long and hard before you allow smoking in the room. You have little to gain and a lot to lose.

TIP #9   Where Did You Get Those Big Blue Eyes and Tent Cards

The blue eyes came from daddy and the tent cards came from cutting manila folders in half.

TIP #10   If You're the Last To Go, There Won't Be a Line

Don't head for the rest room at the start of a break. There will be a line and you'll waste your time. Hang around in the meeting room. Some folks from your audience will want to talk with you—some will have questions. This is an excellent opportunity to get feedback on how it's going. It's also a good time to talk privately with any troublemakers.

Speaking of trouble–see Tip #10A.

TIP #10A Nothing Is Ever as Simple as It Sounds

Take the coffee break, for example. A lot of people don't like coffee. They want decaffeinated or tea. Of the tea drinkers, some want sugar, and some want lemon. Of the sugar users some want regular, and some want low-cal.

And there can be more trouble at the coffee break. Tip #10B tells you how.

TIP #10B Don't Have a Traffic Jam at the Coffee Pot

You will if you don't have the right sequence. Place the cups *before* the coffee, not after. And put the cream and sugar and other supplies on a table separate from the coffee. That will relieve congestion and smooth the flow.

TIP #11 How to Have Your Cake and Eat It, Too— Or How to Start on Time Without Starting on Time

Start the meeting on time with a 3-to-5-minute slide show of famous, interesting, humorous, and provocative quotes. (See examples in the Hot Spice chapter.) That gives the audience another three to five minutes to assemble and settle down before the main event. (And you *did* start on time.)

TIP #12 You Can Leave Your Bow at Home, But Bring Your Own Arrows

Signs with arrows pointing in the direction of your meeting will be appreciated by your audience. But not just any sign. First impressions count. Signs with your company name and logo that are professional in appearance will always create a good first impression.

That's a very different impression from signs made at the last minute from a few words and an arrow scrawled in pen on loose-leaf paper.

TIP #13   Some See from the Front, Some See from the Back—If You Do It Twice You'll Get Both Right

It's common to have place cards or tent cards so we'll know who's who. Too often the name is on the front only. If you will put it on both sides, you will make everybody happy. That allows the ones in the back to also see who's who.

TIP #14   How to Make a Pointer in 10 Seconds with Four Rubber Bands

If you travel with your presentation, what are you going to do for a pointer? One answer is the little metal gadget about the size of a tire gauge that telescopes out like a radio aerial to make a pointer. I guess they're all right. I just never trusted anybody that used one. In addition, if you are the least bit nervous, the slightest quiver of your fingers will be amplified by a factor of 10. So instead of having a slight quiver in the hand it will look like you have Saint Vitas' dance by the time it gets to the end of the pointer.

A better solution is to make your own pointer on the spot. Tear off three blank pages of flip-chart paper, roll them up very tight, and distribute four rubber bands up and down the shaft. Makes a perfect pointer without the Saint Vitas' dance. If you have another few seconds you can take a magic marker and color the pointer blue.

Note: Do not color the six inches at the bottom where you grip the pointer. If you do, you'll end up with a blue hand.

TIP #15   Need a Room? Call the Bank

Many banks and savings and loans have community meeting rooms. More often than not, they're free. Also available are meeting rooms at the main public library, and even at some branches of the public library. Other possibilities for finding meeting rooms are lodges and fraternal organizations, shopping centers, and auditoriums at private schools.

TIP #16   Don't Dot the I's and Cross the T's

Round off those big numbers. The detail will only confuse and make it hard to remember. So $501,247.00 becomes $500,000, and $998,482.00 becomes a million dollars. Don't mess around with odd-lots.

TIP #17   When to Use What

Use graphs for sales figures, financial time series, or any set of numbers for which you want to show the trend over a period of time. No more than two or three lines on a graph, please.

If you have to show a complicated graph with many lines, use transparent overlays. That makes it easy for the audience to follow one thing at a time, and you get the benefit of a better understood composite chart when you finish.

Use pie charts to show the distribution of a whole into its component parts. Examples are: budgets, market share, income sources, expense analysis, and so forth. No more than 8 or 10 divisions please. Lump small ones together and call them miscellaneous.

Use bar charts to represent quantity by the length (if horizontal) or height (if vertical). These are also effective when used in conjunction with color coding to show comparisons, such as this year versus last year. Use tables to show things like a mileage/distance chart or timetables. Circle several examples to talk about that illustrate your point.

TIP #18   If You're Out of Date, You're Out to Lunch

Nothing will destroy your credibility quicker than to use out-of-date facts and figures. And for heaven's sake, don't apologize for obsolete numbers. Get them current, and do it now. Sorry about those harsh words—but this is important.

TIP #19   Let's Do It in Living Color

Most presentations are done in black and white.

How drab, dreary, and depressing can you get? Hollywood

learned a better way 30 years ago. Add life and excitement to your presentation by doing it in color. After all, does it take any longer to do it in color? Of course not. Does it cost any more? Maybe a dime or a dollar.

Again, the quality of your presentation is a mirror image of the quality of your firm, your product, your service, your support, and *you*. So make yourself a breed apart. Be first class by going first class with color.

There are two problems with color. The first one is covered in Tip #19A.

TIP #19A   A Rainbow Is Pretty in the Sky But Not on the Screen

Six or eight colors on a single flip, foil, or slide is too much of a good thing. So limit your colors to two or three. But look out for Tip #19B.

TIP #19B   Some Are Better Than Others—Colors, That Is

Choose your colors carefully. Some colors are difficult to see from the back of the room. For example, colors like pink, orange, and yellow are no-no's—they just don't show up well.

The final tip on color is subtle, but has the impact of a sledge hammer. Straight ahead to 20.

TIP #20   Red Stands for Stop, Danger, and Blood

After all, stop signs are red, fire trucks are red, high voltage signs are red. So when you show a slide, a transparency, or write on a flip chart, do it in red to indicate danger, a problem, or the competition. Color coding can complement and enhance the point you are making.

TIP #21   There Is No Substitute for the Real Thing

A 30-second demonstration is more effective than 30 minutes of words. The best method of proving a point, validating a theory, or convincing the skeptic is a demonstration.

If you would like to have a lot of fun, pretend you have never seen a cigarette. Then have someone hand you an unopened pack and ask them to explain to you *with words only* how to open the pack, extract a cigarette, put the right end in the mouth, light it, and smoke.

TIP #22   How Big a Screen Do You Need?

Answer: The distance from the audience to the screen should be no more than six times the width of the projected image.

TIP #23   A Minute Is Too Long But a Millisecond Is Just Right

As soon as you show a new slide or transparency, allow a millisecond or two for the visual impact to sink in. Then explain in general terms what the graph or chart is going to show, any assumptions that are made, and an explanation of the X and Y axes.

TIP #24   You Can Spot the Difference Between an Amateur and a Professional Before You See The First Slide

When the amateur turns the projector on, the audience is hit with a glaring bright light that fills the screen. The same thing happens to the amateur after the last slide. The professional eliminates the glaring light by putting a blank, opaque slide at the beginning and end of the presentation.

TIP #25   The Presenter's First Aid Kit, Or Don't Get Caught with Your Lights Out

You only need one item in your first-aid kit—a spare bulb. The day will come when it will save your life. Well, maybe not your life, but at the time it will sure seem like it.

TIP #26   Don't Get Caught Saying, "Next Slide, Please"

If a football coach can run an entire game from the sidelines using visual signals, surely to goodness you can work out one visual signal to tell your associate when to change slides or transparencies.

TIP #27   Let the Spotlights Help You—Not Hurt You

Many of the rooms you will be in will have recessed spotlights in the ceiling. Be sure to position your screen to keep the spotlights off the screen. But position your flip-chart stand to have a spotlight on it. Careful now, a few inches can make a big difference. That roll at the top of a flip chart projects out slightly and can cast a shadow half way down the flip chart. If you move it six inches you can solve the problem.

TIP #28   Never, Never, Never Pack and Ship Your Presentation

The only thing worse than being up the creek without a paddle is being at the meeting without your presentation. That's what will happen to you if you pack your presentation in your luggage and check it at the airport. That's the time your luggage will get lost. There is only one answer. Always hand-carry your presentation.

TIP #29   Everybody Loves Cartoons

So keep your eyes open for cartoons that you can use in your presentation to highlight and emphasize a point. They will add a little spice or at least some salt and pepper to your presentation.

TIP #30   KISS—"Keep It Simple, Stupid"

Complex charts or graphs that make multiple points at the same time may be clever to create, but they are confusing to your audience.

And watch those complex words. See Tip #30A.

Dunagin's people

'I lost a fortune in the stock market today . . . yours.'

FIGURE 12A Keep your eyes open for cartoons to illustrate your points. They add spice to the presentation.

TIP #30A KISS—Version #2

Don't use technical words, industry language, or phrases and acronyms that would not be well known to your audience. If any are central to your presentation, use them, but be sure you define them first.

TIP #31 Never Play with a Full Deck

Never walk in a room in full view of the audience with an armload of two or three hours' worth of material. Worse still is stacking the entire presentation on a table in the front of the room. If you do, the audience will be preoccupied with the size of the stack and how much longer is left to go. "What do you think, Joe?" "Looks to me like another two or three hours."

When you arrive early, what you want to do is hide all of the presentation material except for enough material to carry you to the first break.

TIP #32   Use the Magic of the Circle

If you have a lot of transparencies, or slides with a lot of words, you can make them more interesting and more readable by breaking them up. The use of simple circles, rectangles, arrows, and so on can enhance the appearance and the interest of words.

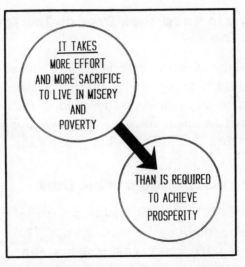

FIGURE 12B Simple circles and arrows
can enhance your message.

TIP #33   50 Percent of the Time You Don't Need a Screen

All you need is a light-colored wall to project on. Just set the pictures that are hanging on the wall down on the floor and you're in business.

TIP #34   A Portable Emergency Screen

The only problem with projecting on a wall is that sometimes there will be wallpaper with a design—like red roses. You can't project on red-rose wallpaper.

That's where the emergency kit comes in. The emergency kit consists of four pieces of blank flip-chart paper and a roll of masking tape. It will only take about 20 seconds to tape in place a temporary screen of flip-chart paper. Always use masking tape, never Scotch tape. The red roses will come off with the Scotch tape and you will have to pay for repapering a wall.

TIP #35   How to Keep Their Eyes on The Target— And on You, Too

You can control the audience by establishing a format on a flip chart or chalkboard for the presentation and the discussion.

A structured format will keep the mind of the audience on the target, save time, and help you accomplish your objective.

Check out Figure 12C and see what you think.

TIP #36   Don't Get Caught in the Dark

If it hasn't happened to you yet, it's just a matter of time. Just as you get into your presentation, the lights go out. That's not a malfunction. Some misguided good samaritan has turned the lights out, thinking they are doing you a favor. They come from the old school that says any time you project anything on a screen—turn the lights out. They don't realize that modern overhead projections are designed to be seen with the lights on, and that you want them on so you can have eye contact and group participation.

So before you start, check out the location of the light switches so you can have light on the audience, light on the subject, and light on yourself.

TIP #37   He Can Sell Your Product Better Than You Can

The person who can sell your product better than you can yourself is the satisfied user. So preplan at a strategic point in the presenta-

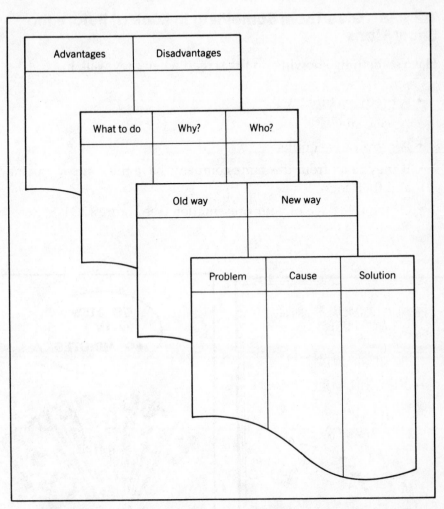

FIGURE 12C A structured format will keep the mind on the target.

tion to call on a satisfied user to give a testimonial. Two or three would be even better.

If they can't be there, play a tape cassette of their testimonials. If you don't have that, show pictures of them and give their testimonials for them.

TIP #38   Give Them Something to Look at Before the Show Starts

Have something showing on the screen when they walk in.

- A pretty picture
- A welcome
- A provocative quote
- If they're all from the same company, have the company name and their logo
- Or the title page of your presentation (see Figure 12D)

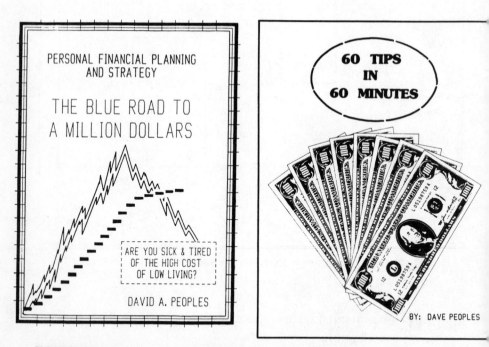

FIGURE 12D Have something showing on the screen when they walk in—like the title page of your presentation.

TIP #39 If You Say It Again, Say It Differently

There's nothing wrong with repeating something for emphasis. But don't say it the same way. Say it a different way.

TIP #40 Emily Post Says, "Don't Point"

You shouldn't, either. So avoid that tendency to point when you want to call on someone. Instead, extend your hand, fingers together and palm up. And please, don't ever point to someone with a pointer.

TIP #41 If You Tend to Scream and Shout. . . .

Remember these words of wisdom: "People will believe anything if you whisper it."

TIP #42 It's Okay to Ship Your Handouts If . . .

. . . you hand carry an original copy with you. Then if things go wrong and your handouts get lost, a fast copy center can put you back in business.

TIP #43 Don't Let the Holes Show Through

If you use a sheet of three-ring binder paper for the revelation technique, the holes will show on the screen. It looks really tacky. A better choice is blank copier paper with no holes. This can also serve double duty by being your cheat sheet.

TIP #44 A Tilt Forward Will Make It Straight

When you project up to a large screen the projected image is wider at the top of the screen than it is at the bottom. Some people refer to this as the keystone effect.

The solution is to tilt the top of the screen forward. That will square it up perpendicular to the projected light. Some screens are designed to do that. Check the supporting framework of the screen.

If it looks different from any you've ever seen, then I betcha it will tilt at the top. Sometimes screens that pull down from the ceiling are designed to push back at the bottom and fasten to the wall—the result is the same.

TIP #45   Make a One-Time Decision

Are you going to stand to the right or to the left of the overhead projector? Don't mix it up. Make a one-time decision and always stand on that side. You'll be more comfortable if you do.

FYI, most right-handed people feel more comfortable standing to the left of the projector as they face it.

While we're making decisions, go on to Tip #45A.

TIP #45A   Make Another One-Time Decision

When you lay your transparencies beside the projector, are you going to turn them from left to right or from right to left? Make a one-time decision and do it the same way every time. If you don't, the time will come when you forget where you are and what comes next. This is the same as hitting the backward button of the slide projector instead of the forward. By the way, you can solve *that* problem by taping the hand-held control gadget to the top of the table so that the forward button is always toward you.

TIP #46   Turn It Off When Not in Use

The projector, that is. Here's the problem. The human eye is naturally drawn toward bright light. If you leave the projector on when you are not using it, the eyes will be drawn to the light, and the ears will be drawn to your voice. The eyes will win and the ears will lose. You can solve the problem by eliminating the contention. Just turn off the projector.

TIP #47   Do Your Filing on Your Own Time— Not the Audience's Time

Have you ever seen this? The presenter walks to the front with a three-ring binder containing his or her transparencies. He pops open the binder, removes and shows the first transparency. Now comes the problem. He attempts to refile the transparency in the binder with one hand. It seems like it takes forever. I think the audience can legitimately say, "Do your filing on your own time, not on our time."

TIP #48   Use Your Pen For a Pointer

If you have a large audience and a large screen, a standard pointer won't reach the full screen. The solution is to use your pen directly on the transparency itself. Don't try to hold it in midair—it will quiver and shake. Drop the pen on the transparency, move the point to where you want it, then remove your hand.

As a by-product, this technique allows you to always be facing the audience, not the screen.

TIP #49   What's Hard with One Can Be Easy with Two

Overhead projectors, that is. This allows you to have the big picture on one projector while you review and show the component parts on the second. That way you can show the forest and the trees at the same time. Very good for complex subjects.

TIP #50   How to Separate the Few from the Many

If you end up with a transparency full of numbers, use a felt-tip pen to circle the few you want to talk about. If you use different colored pens to circle numbers, you can refer to them by color. Sure makes it a lot easier to follow.

TIP #51   How to Make Black and White Look Like a Sunrise

If you are handed a canned pitch with black and white transparencies, you can change them to beautiful color in two seconds. You do this by overlaying the black and white transparencies with a blank colored transparency. Just three or four different colored blank transparencies can make the presentation look like a sunrise.

TIP #52 If You Can Read It on the Floor, You've Got It Just Right

Is the lettering on your transparencies too small to be seen from the back of the room? Place it on the floor. If you can read it while standing up, it's probably large enough.

TIP #53 A Rubber Band Will Keep the Flips Off the Floor

A common design of flip-chart stands is to have two metal posts that correspond to the holes in your flip-chart paper. Trouble is, when you turn the pages the paper has a tendency to buckle in the middle or fall off one or both of the metal posts. A simple solution is to loop two rubber bands together and stretch them across both metal posts. One won't reach across, but two will do the job.

TIP #54 How to Preserve, Protect, and Defend Your Flip Charts

One of the problems with flip charts is that they tend to get beaten up and dog-eared, especially if you travel with them. You can triple their life span with a little tender loving care. Here's how.

Get a cardboard tube to carry them in. (The kind with a plastic lid that fits on both ends.) You want the tube to be slightly longer than your flip charts are wide. An excess of about one inch on each end will be fine. You can get these tubes at an art supply or office supply store—or check your own mail room.

Now lay your flip charts on the floor face down on top of two or three sheets of blank paper. Position the blank sheets so that they are slightly off square to your presentation flip charts. Now roll them up to fit into the tube. Please note that if the blank sheets are slightly off square, there will be excess paper hanging over each end when you roll it up. But the excess paper will be the blank paper. Note also that you are rolling up your presentation backward. This will eliminate the curling up at the bottom when you put them on a flip-chart stand.

Now we Scotch tape one of the plastic lids in place. We wad up two or three pieces of paper towels and drop them down the tube. Slide the rolled-up presentation into the tube on top of the wadded-up paper towels. Place more wadded-up paper towels in the open end and Scotch tape the other plastic lid in place. That's it. You now have your presentation safe and secure for travel.

TIP #55   An Accident Waiting to Happen

Sooner or later you are going to be walking up to give a presentation and drop the whole show on the floor. It's bad enough picking up your foils, but the really bad news is that they are now out of sequence and you don't remember for sure what went where.

The first-aid for this kind of disaster is to be sure you have numbered the material sequentially so you can easily reassemble it. And speaking of disaster, make an extra copy of your presentation and keep it locked away somewhere. Some day you'll be glad you did.

TIP #56   Don't Fiddle and Fumble with the Flip Charts

Have you ever seen the next speaker trying to get their flip charts threaded on the metal post? Two or three fit on one side while two or three are dropping off the other. What a mess. Seems like it takes forever. That will make a nervous wreck out of anybody.

You can solve this problem in advance by having your flip charts held together with two of the large paper-clip-type clamps at the top. The holes are prealigned and the entire unit (clamps intact) is slipped over the metal post.

TIP #57   How to Preserve, Protect, and Defend Your Transparencies

You can do this by inserting them in the standard three-ring binder acetate protective folder. They still project just fine.

TIP #58   Practice Your Swing

If you're not experienced in flip-chart presentations, you need to practice swinging the charts back over the top of the flip-chart stand. Sometimes it's not as easy as you might think.

TIP #59   How to Find One Among Many

If you are drawing charts as you go, or are using them as your alternate medium, you might want to refer back to a particular chart. That's a technique of relating a future point to a past principle. It ties the presentation together and makes the conclusions more acceptable since the logic is better established.

The problem is, how do you find the page you want to turn back to?

Here's the answer. When you are explaining the chart the first time just turn the corner down before you turn the chart over, just like you would the page of a book. Then when you want to find that chart, turn all the charts back over to their original positions. The one with the corner turned down will stand out.

TIP #60   Start with a Clean Slate

You can do this by cleaning the top of the overhead projector. Here's the deal.

I promise you, every overhead projector you walk up to will be dirty. The top of the glass will project fingerprints, lint, smudge marks, spilled coffee, and who knows what.

Here's the solution. Since you will have to go to the bathroom many times before the presentation anyway, just bring back some paper towels the next trip. Five dry ones in one hand, and five soggy, wet ones in the other. Then clean the top of the glass just like it was the windshield of your car.

The nonverbal communication says, "I'm a professional and this is a quality show—you deserve the best." (At the very least, a clean slate.)

Next thing you know, your colleagues will start cleaning their slates too. Quality is contagious. Pass it on.

CHAPTER 13

Rehearse, Rehearse, Rehearse—Then Cheat

Good presenters communicate the feeling that they are comfortable, relaxed, in command of the situation, know what they are talking about, and enjoy doing what they are doing.

Are they born that way? Do they just wake up one morning with those traits? How does it happen? I suggest to you that one becomes a good presenter the same way one becomes a good golfer, a good cabinetmaker, or a good lawyer. By preparation, by practice, and by doing.

The good golfer makes it look so easy. The smooth swing, the distance, the accuracy. More than easy, it looks effortless. But behind that superb coordination of mind and muscle are years of work, practice, and a few gallons of sweat. There is no easy and painless path to golfing goodness. If you want to get there you have to pay your dues.

And so it is with the presenter. The good ones make it look so easy, so natural. They appear calm, composed, and confident. They come through to the audience as having warmth, authority, and sincerity. But behind that appearance are hours of preparation, practice, and doing. As in golf, there is no easy and painless path to becoming a good presenter. But there is a simple way. It's called rehearse, rehearse, rehearse.

Would you think making a presentation is more like an art or more like a science? Most people would agree that it is more like an art. That being the case, as is true of all forms of art, you improve with practice. And the *only* way to improve is by practice.

There are two compelling reasons for you to rehearse. The first is that it is the single best solution to the problem of tight nerves and sweaty palms. You have good reason to be nervous and sweaty if you don't know what you're going to say, or how you're going to say it. The concept of, "I'll play it by ear" is an example of both stupidity and a cop-out for not doing your homework. It is a guarantee of mediocrity at best.

The second reason for rehearsing is even more important than the first. It has to do with achieving your objective. Let's suppose that the objective of the presentation is to sell something—a product, a service, or what have you. Let's further suppose that on a scale from zero to 100 percent that your presentation effectiveness is 50 percent and your competitor's effectiveness is 100 percent. Are you going to get 50 percent of the business? Absolutely not. You are going to get zero. Your competitor is going to get all the business. Every time you do battle with that competitor you are going to lose. The win/lose decision is not an analogue decision—it is binary. Most prospects or clients are not in the business of helping the needy. A very important key to being a winner on the competitive battlefield is to give an effective presentation. Some say it is the *most* important key.

What about price? Isn't the low bidder always the winner? If that were true, we could eliminate a few million sales jobs. Let's take the computer business. Studies have been done that rank the buying criteria for experienced computer users. In those studies price ranks last.

So if you could use a little more business, get your act together, do your homework and rehearse, rehearse, rehearse. The quality of your presentation tells your prospect the quality of your product, or the quality of your service.

Let's talk about a few specifics. If you have not rehearsed—if you are not sure what you are going to say, and you have to switch your brain into a deep-think mode to think up what you're going to say next in front of the audience—then you cannot have good eye contact with the audience. It is impossible to have eye contact while in deep-think mode. If you are in deep thought, what are you looking at? You are looking at the floor, the ceiling, or out into space with glazed-over eyes.

Another example. We have talked about the importance of a pleasant facial expression—specifically, a smile. If you have not rehearsed, you're not sure what you're going to say next. If you have to switch into deep-think mode to think up what you're going to say next, what is going to be the expression of your face? Not only will it not be a smile, it will be a frown. Nothing could be worse. It is impossible to smile and deep-think at the same time. And by the way, what do you think would be the tone of your voice? You've got it—a monotone.

A major problem with presenters is that they are so content-oriented, so absorbed in what they are saying, that they are oblivious to how they appear to the audience. If you have glazed-over eyes, a frown on your face, and are speaking in a monotone, it doesn't matter how good your content. There is no way you can keep the attention and interest of the audience and achieve your objective. You will lose.

The only way you can concentrate on your voice, your facial expression, and have eye contact with the audience, is to have a free mind to concentrate on those items. The only way you can have a free mind is to know in advance what you are going to say. The only way you can do that is to rehearse.

There is a right way and a wrong way to rehearse. The wrong way is to just flip through your visuals and glance at your cheat sheets.

The right way to rehearse is to duplicate the conditions of your presentations. That means rehearsing in the actual room using the actual visual aids, going through the actual movements, gestures, and saying the actual words. There is no substitute for doing the real thing, the real way. If you don't, I assure you there will be some surprises in store for you when you are standing in front of a live audience. And the last thing you want or need is a surprise.

If your rehearsal can be made to some friends or colleague, so much the better. Ask for their specific suggestions for improvement—they are more likely to see the forest in addition to the trees.

If your presentation involves writing on a flip chart or a board, be sure to include that in your rehearsal. This will allow you to solve in advance the problems of:

- Spelling
- Positioning
- Running off the page
- Running out of paper
- Out-of-ink Magic Marker
- No chalk
- Lettering too small
- Poor drawing
- Out of scale
- No color
- No erasers

That gives us an idea of the things that can go wrong—and that's just in one area. There are three important things to remember. The first is, there is no substitute for a dress rehearsal. The second is, there is no substitute for a dress rehearsal. And the third is, there is no substitute for a dress rehearsal.

The ultimate fear of all presenters is not that they will stumble and fumble (bad as that is) through a presentation, but that they will be standing in front of an audience and suddenly go blank. Some even have dreams about that and wake up in a cold sweat.

If we follow the simple steps of the Blueprint for Success, that will never happen. The purpose of the cheat sheet is to guide us step-by-step through the presentation. It gives us key words and phrases; questions to ask; and miniature drawings of pictures, graphs, schematics, and so on. It has the first three to five words we will say for each visual. It is a shorthand script of the presentation and tells us what to do and when.

If we have done a proper job of rehearsing, we will have become very familiar with our cheat sheets and the material they contain. A quick glance at a cheat sheet tells you where you are and what comes next. With practice, one glance will carry you for two to three minutes, or longer. What happens here is that when you glance at the cheat sheet you pick up the first three to five words and any key words that go with the next visual. Then when you say those words, if you have properly rehearsed, the follow-on words and explanation will flow automatically and smoothly.

A strange thing will happen after you have given a presentation a few times. Your mind will start to form a mental image of the cheat sheet. Next thing you know you will be able to see the cheat sheets in your mind without looking at them. At a minimum, one quick glance at a cheat sheet will bring a recall of the entire page.

This gives you the reality of the dream of all presenters:

- You have the power and drama of key words and phrases.
- The surrounding words flow automatically and smoothly.
- You convey the appearance of giving an effective and exciting presentation extemporaneously and from memory.

CHEAT SHEET

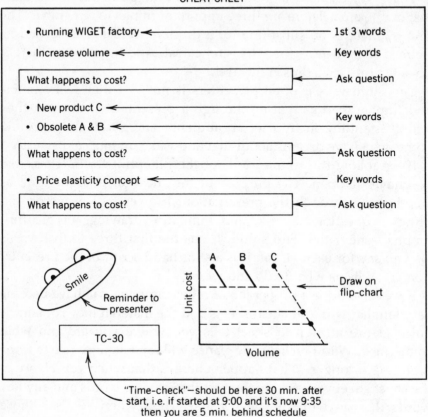

FIGURE 13A Sample of a cheat sheet.

Cheat sheets take many forms and different media depending on the presenter and his or her choice of visual aids. For example:

- Around the sides of frames used for transparencies.
- Lightly written and drawn on flip charts.
- A page underneath each transparency.
- On the transparency itself if you use the material known as Retrophane. (This is opaque material that allows you to have notes on the transparency itself.)

- Flip frames (side panel attached to a transparency that folds out and functions as frame and as cheat sheets.)
- On the back of the previous page of a flip chart.

There is another technique of cheating I stumbled onto that is effective and dramatic.

In giving my presentation on "How to Give an Effective Presentation," I talk about becoming a professional cheater by using cheat sheets. I further describe how the mind will form a mental image of the cheat sheet, and your memory will improve.

At this point I inject some Hot Spice as follows:

In fact, just talking about improving your memory will improve your memory. Let me demonstrate what I mean.

- Right here by the side of the door we have a *washing* machine.
- Behind this picture (I am going down the left side of the room) there is an *atom* bomb.
- Back there in the corner stands a *chef*.
- On the table in the back of the room is a bunch of *medicine* bottles.
- Beside the medicine is a stack of *money* to pay for the medicine.
- In that corner is another *atom* bomb.
- Underneath that window (I am coming back up the right side) is a *jack*—like a car jack.
- Here in the front of the room is parked a *van*.
- And here on the floor in the center of the room is *hair*—like a barber shop.
- Finally up on the ceiling are *tiles*.

"Now to demonstrate how much your memory has improved, let's altogether see if we can name the items."

I now point to each position and the group responds with the correct answer. They always get it right and it loosens up the audience.

I then congratulate them on their memory improvement and ask who would like to volunteer to name the first 10 Presidents of the

United States. That brings dead silence. I say, "Wait a minute. Every person in this room can name the first 10 Presidents of the United States. The first President was (point to washing machine) Washington, the second President was (atom bomb) Adams, the third President was (chef) Jefferson, then (medicine) Madison, then (money) Monroe, then (atom bomb) another Adams, then (jack) Jackson, then (van) Van Buren, then (hair) Harrison, then (tile) Tyler.

Well, that's a lot of fun and the audience gets a kick out of it.

I, of course, had a cheat sheet like Figure 13B (just in case I ever needed it).

One night I had a nightmare and woke up in a cold sweat. I was doing this memory exercise, and right in the middle of it my mind went blank. I said uh, ah, looked up at the ceiling as panic set in, and finally looked down at my cheat sheet. Well, it was clear to the audience what had happened, and also clear that I was looking down at my notes. What a nightmare. What could be worse than to have a memory lapse in the middle of a memory demonstration and have to look at your notes?

For weeks that bothered me. I couldn't get it out of my mind. I just knew that some day it was going to happen for real. What was I going to do?

Then I got to thinking about one of the best speakers I know. More in demand than most. Always the highlight of any convention. Always got a standing ovation. He was different from all the others. He never used a podium. He walked to the front of the stage and spoke for 40 minutes without notes or prompts. Great movement across the front of the stage and dramatic gestures as he moved first one arm in front of his body toward the audience and then the other. You would have thought you were in a theater on Broadway watching a professional performance. How did he do it? How could he talk for 40 minutes without notes or prompts, and rattle off statistical volumes, dates, and dollars?

Then one day it came to me. Those arm movements toward the audience were more than a gesture. The back of the hand was always facing the audience. With every gesture, I think he was reading his notes written on the palms of his hands.

What a clever idea. I now make cheat notes of the first 10 Presi-

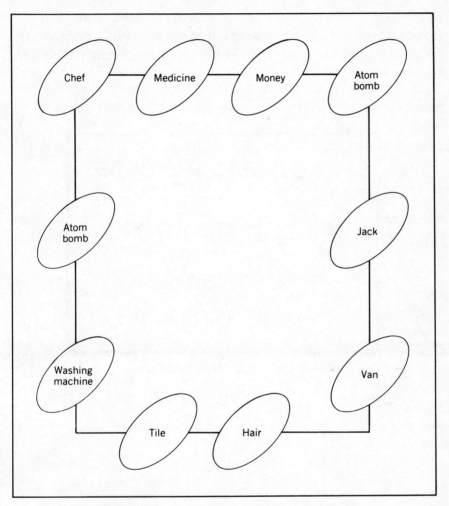

FIGURE 13B Cheat sheet for memory exercise.

dents on the palms of my hands. I haven't had to use them (yet), but I sure sleep better.

The added value of notes in the hand is that you have freedom of movement. It frees you from the restriction of standing where you can refer to your cheat sheets. One thing you might consider is the use of a few notes (like some heavy statistics) on your palm in addition to your cheat sheets. That way you can walk away from your notes and rattle off a whole series of numbers, volumes, dates, and so forth. That'll really impress them—just as my friend did with the facts on his fingers.

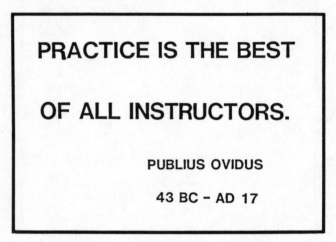

PRACTICE IS THE BEST

OF ALL INSTRUCTORS.

PUBLIUS OVIDUS

43 BC – AD 17

FIGURE 13C Some things never change.

CHAPTER 14

GETTING
THEM BACK
FROM THE
BREAK

If there is any bigger problem than getting them back from the break, I don't know what it is. If your scheduled 15-minute break turns into 30 minutes, and you have two breaks in the morning and two in the afternoon, you have lost an hour of time on your schedule.

Before we talk about solving that problem, let's talk about the frequency of breaks. You should never go for two hours without a break. On the other hand, if you take a break in less than an hour, you are not making efficient use of your time or the audience's time. The right time for a break lies somewhere between those two extremes.

However, the breaks should be planned in conjunction with the duration of a presentation. For example, suppose your presentation takes 1 hour and 45 minutes. Should you take a break after 45 minutes? I think not. A better plan is to identify a specific place in the presentation where you could have the audience take a stand-up stretch while you continue the presentation. A good place to do this is where you tell a joke, a story, a personal experience, or so forth. For example, you might say, "Let me tell you a personal experience that illustrates the point we're talking about. While I do, why don't we all stand up and stretch our legs." That's smooth, flows well, and seems to be naturally built into the presentation. Don't forget to invite them to sit back down at the end of your story.

Let's take another example. Suppose you have a 30-minute presentation that follows a 45-minute presentation with no break in between. Even though the elapsed time is only 1 hour, 15 minutes, you will be well advised to ask the audience to take an in-place 60-second stretch before you start.

That will wake them up, get the juices flowing, and psychologically reset the audience to zero in preparation for your presentation. You need to force a mental break from the first presentation. A stand-up stretch will help to do that.

The absolutely worst way to have a break is to be motoring through your presentation, look down at your watch, and suddenly announce, "Oh my goodness, I didn't realize what time it is—would you like to take a break?" On the contrary, breaks need to be planned and built into your presentation at specific and strategic points.

The next rule is to have everybody on the same time. If there is a clock on the wall you might suggest that they set their watches to the time of the wall clock. If there is no wall clock, ask them to set their watches to your watch.

The next rule is: Don't announce the duration of the break. Instead announce the start-back time. For example, don't say, "Let's take a 10-minute break," but, "Let's take a break and we'll start back at 10:33." Make it an odd time and write it on a flip chart. That will put the focus on when you are going to start. If you just announce a 10-minute break, people won't remember when the 10 minutes started.

Everyday millions of people turn on the T.V. soap operas. Some people will plan their entire day around *The Edge of Night*. How do the networks get people to do that? They do it by giving the audience a compelling reason to tune back in. Just before the break (yesterday), they built up to an emotional event, a trauma, a surprise, an unanswered question with the burning issue, "Is Suzie really pregnant?"

In our own way we need to do the same thing in planning our break. It needs to be strategically placed in the presentation at a point of high interest. We will provide the answer right after the break. We also need to give the audience a preview of coming attractions. For example, in my financial presentation I say, "When we return from the break, we will examine the real truth about your broker, your banker, and your financial advisor." When presenting the material contained in this book I say, "When we return from the break, we will examine the Seven Deadly Sins—seven guaranteed ways to give a dull, dry, and boring presentation." Those are subjects that have both an intellectual and emotional interest to the audience. We should plan our breaks around the high points of our presentation.

But the break is not a stand-alone event. If the presentation should have started at 9:00, and you started 10 minutes late, that sends a message to the audience that you will also start late after the break. You pay the price in more ways than one if you don't start on time.

On the other hand, if you started your presentation on time, then you have signaled the audience that you will also start on time after the break.

Another technique for getting them back from the break is to anticipate their needs and requirements. In my company, for example, people head for the phones at the break. They want to call in, check in, and see if there are any fires burning back at the ranch. Well, there is no way you can take a 10-minute break and get them back from the phones. So you might think the answer is to take a longer break. Possibly, but there is a better answer. If the meeting lasts a half-day, you can announce up front that there will be a 10-minute break and a 20-minute break. You further state that the intent of the long break is to give the attendees time to call the office. That way, the total break time is no greater than if you had two 15-minute breaks, but the breaks are better planned to meet the needs of the audience.

Another technique for getting them back from the break is to get their agreement on how long the break should be. Here's the way this works. When you come to the place in the presentation where you have planned the break, you announce to the group that you are going to take a break. You would then state that this is their meeting and ask them how long a break they want. You might prompt them by saying, "Ten minutes?" "Fifteen minutes?" Someone will volunteer a number like "Ten minutes." You then ask the audience, "Is 10 minutes all right? Does anybody have a problem with 10 minutes?" If there is no response you can announce the time the meeting will resume (10 minutes later).

What has happened here is that you have established a psychological gentlemen's agreement. Since no one objected to the 10 minutes, and you gave them the opportunity to do just that, your audience will tend to feel compelled to be back on time.

Another technique is to do what they do at the theater, the opera, and the symphony. During the intermission, blink the house lights and the hall lights off and on to announce that the show is about to begin.

Or you can play dirty pool and show a short movie right after the break. That gives you an excuse to close the doors and keep them closed. Anyone who does try to get in is faced with a pitch black room, must stumble over people, and may end up sitting in somebody's lap. I assure you, at the next break they will be back on time.

Continuing with the psychological warfare strategy, there is another thing you can do at the start of the meeting that sends a powerful message to the audience. The message you send is, "This is a business meeting and it's going to be run like a business meeting." The way you send that message is to keep the meeting room doors closed until the exact time the meeting is to start. Then you open the doors and let the audience in. Many people have never experienced that, but they sure understand the message.

A final tip on breaks is to make a visual aid that shows the location of the restrooms, phones, coffee, and so on. This will save both you and them time and questions. In the design of the visual aid you can leave space to write-in the restart time. They will be impressed with your foresight, planning, and thoughtfulness.

CHAPTER 15

Time Control

The great enemy of all meetings, conferences, seminars, and presentations is time. How many meetings have you ever attended that finished early?

Here's the kind of thing that happens. The meeting starts 10 minutes late. The introductions take 15 minutes instead of 5. The welcome takes 15 instead of 10. The first speaker takes 50 instead of the 35 he was scheduled for. The first coffee break lasts 20 minutes instead of 10, and so on.

You are scheduled to be on the program at 4:00. Well, by that time the meeting is more than an hour behind schedule and there's another speaker ahead of you who has not yet been introduced.

That brings us to Rule #1: Get on the program early in the day. Not only is the audience fresher, more attentive, and more interested—you also avoid all the things that can go wrong during the day.

Rule #2 is: Don't contribute to the problem. The hallmark of a good presenter is the ability to control and manage time. A good presenter will always finish on time. A good presenter can even finish in less than the scheduled time. It is quite common for the host running a seminar to ask a speaker if it is possible to finish a little early and help make up some time. A good presenter will say, "Yes, when would you like me to finish?" Within reasonable limits a good presenter can finish when he or she wants to finish. How?

First let's talk about what tends to happen to the inexperienced presenter who is not well prepared and has not rehearsed.

About 45 minutes into an allotted one hour, the inexperienced presenter finally notices what time it is, realizes there is only 15 minutes left, and that he or she isn't even halfway through the presentation. The instinctive reaction is to rush through the remaining material and set a new world's record for words-per-minute.

Rushing is worse than ineffective. It causes an adverse reaction. The audience becomes uncomfortable with the rush, the pace, and the rapid-fire words. Additionally, the close—which is the most important part of the presentation—is rushed through and completely loses its impact and effectiveness. The presenter has become his or her own worst enemy. Rushing is self-defeating. People will remember not *what* was said but *how long* it took to say it.

The experienced presenter will have anticipated the requirement for time control. As part of the planning and construction of the presentation, he or she will have created a *modular outline* of the key elements of the presentation. In Figure 15A we see an example of how that might look.

This particular presentation is made up of five logical components: A, B, C, D, and E. Think of these as minichapters. Two of them (B and D) are further broken down into subheadings within a chapter.

The second step for the experienced presenter comes as a by-product of rehearsing. A record is made of the time it takes to complete each component of the presentation.

The third and final step is to evaluate the relative value and contribution of each component to achieving the final object, then answer the following question: "If I wanted to reduce my total time by 10 or 15 minutes, what elements would I eliminate, and what would their priorities be?"

In Figure 15A we see that the presenter would eliminate B2, C, and D2. That reduces a one-hour presentation to 45 minutes. The key point is that the presenter has gone through this entire thought process in advance. Thus, when the presenter has a need to cut it short, he or she already knows—in order of priority—what can be eliminated.

We never want to rush through a presentation. Instead, our solution to time constraints is to eliminate elements of the presentation. The audience will never know that anything was eliminated. They will think the presentation was planned to be 45 minutes long.

You will find this difficult to do if you are the person who created the presentation. The pride of ownership and authorship will compel you to think that you have to present it all. But my experience is that the 45-minute presentation goes just as well as the full one-hour version. In fact, I suspect that you will find as I have, that a shorter version often goes better than the longer version. People remember more if you tell them less.

Using this technique, I suggest you complete your presentation five minutes sooner than your scheduled or published time. What a breath of fresh air you will be to your audience. Rarely in the course of a million presentations has anyone finished early. You can be one in a million.

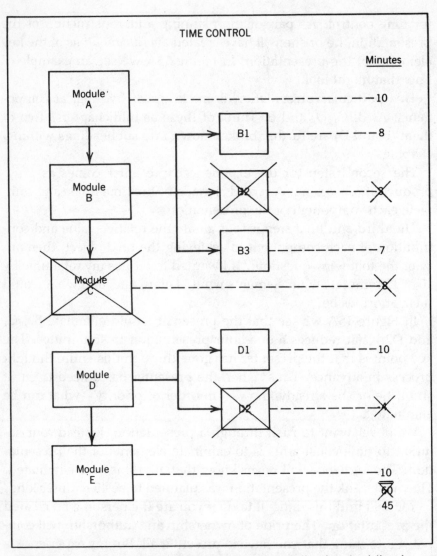

FIGURE 15A We can control the time of a presentation by deciding in advance the priority of things to delete.

Now that we know how to control time, it's important to build in a check point periodically during the presentation. The checkpoint will tell us if we are ahead of schedule or behind schedule.

The way we do this is to figure out in advance exactly where we should be after 15 minutes into the presentation. We then write on our cheat sheet, "TC + 15." This means, "Time check for 15 minutes to get to this point." So if we started at 9:00 A.M. when we get to this cheat sheet it should be 9:15. If it's 9:20 then we know we are 5 minutes behind schedule, and we need to eliminate one of the preplanned elements and make up time. We do the same thing for 30 minutes into the presentation (TC + 30), and for 45 minutes (TC + 45).

You need to know that you will always start at least five minutes later than you think, even if you start on time. Let me explain.

If the program says you start at 9:00, you don't. Even if the audience are in their seats at 9:00, there's always an announcement or two, a question or two, your introduction, and so forth. Then you have to get to the front. By the time you say your first word it will be at least 9:05.

So even though the program says you have an hour (9:00–10:00), we want to plan our presentation for 50 minutes. We lose 5 minutes on the front end, and we want to finish 5 minutes early.

The bottom line is that an hour on the schedule really means a 50-minute presentation. If you want or need one hour, ask for 1 hour and 10 minutes on the schedule.

The worst thing a presenter can do is to be dull, dry, and boring. The second worst thing a presenter can do is run overtime. If you follow these simple techniques, you can finish when you choose to finish.

Comes the Dawn and Sweaty Palms

It may start the night before your presentation. If not, then certainly by the time the sun comes up on the big day you will start to get one or more of the following diseases:

- DEOMOPHOBIA
- LALIOPHOBIA
- KATAGELOPHOBIA

They are:

- Fear of crowds
- Fear of speaking
- Fear of ridicule

The symptoms are:

- Fast pulse
- Shallow breathing
- Muscle spasms that affect the
  —voice
  —knees
  —hands
- Dry mouth
- Cold extremities
- Eyes dilated
- Nausea
- Sweaty palms
- Tight nerves
- Blurred vision

You will be in very good company. Studies have shown that the number one fear of human beings in the United States is speaking before a group. In fact, the study revealed that people fear speaking before a group more than they fear death.

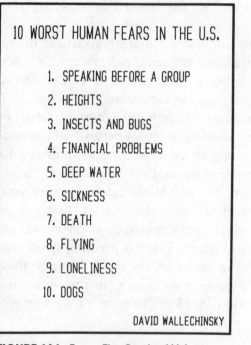

10 WORST HUMAN FEARS IN THE U.S.

1. SPEAKING BEFORE A GROUP
2. HEIGHTS
3. INSECTS AND BUGS
4. FINANCIAL PROBLEMS
5. DEEP WATER
6. SICKNESS
7. DEATH
8. FLYING
9. LONELINESS
10. DOGS

DAVID WALLECHINSKY

FIGURE 16A From *The Book of Lists.*
People fear speaking before a group
more than they fear death.

Don't be surprised if your mind starts wishing for laryngitis, a snowstorm, the flu, an earthquake, a closed airport, or anything that would cancel or postpone the presentation.

What's going on here is both good news and bad news. The bad news is, you will probably never get completely over it. The good news is that everybody has it—entertainers, professional actors, even people who conduct workshops on public speaking. The additional good news is that your presentation will be better because of it. Your mind will be quicker, your movement greater, your gestures stronger. Your sweaty palms are your friends. They are proof positive that you are a normal human being. Normal because it's in your blood and in your genes. You inherited it from your earliest ancestors. Nature has given us the juice to fight or flee in threatening or uncomfortable situations. The juice is adrenaline that automatically pumps into the bloodstream to help you out. So be glad you have it.

We need to understand that nervousness in front of a group is not a physical or psychological deficiency. It is a normal and healthy reaction of the body. What we want to do is to control it and get those butterflies to fly in formation.

The best answer to controlling nervousness is preparation and rehearsal. The adrenaline flows because of uncertainty, lack of confidence, and a fear of the unknown. If you have done a good job of planning, preparation, and rehearsal, then you will have removed the uncertainty. You will be confident because you will know what you are going to say and what you are going to do. You will be in control of yourself, your material, and your visuals. You will have removed the unknown. There is no other good answer.

So let's get this show on the road. The first thing we need to do is arrive at least one hour before our presentation. Believe me, you will be glad you did. Here are some of the things that can and will go wrong:

- The cord of your visual aid equipment won't reach the electrical outlet.
- You finally get an extension cord but your three-pronged plug won't fit into the two-pronged holes of the extension cord.
- The light control for your room is on the other side of the partition in another room.
- There is no space beside the overhead projector for you to lay your transparencies.
- The make and model of the slide projector works very differently from the one you're accustomed to.
- The flip-chart stand is not designed for your flip-chart paper.
- On the hotel's announcement board the name of your program is misspelled and the start time is not correct.
- It's Monday morning and the air conditioning to your room was turned off over the weekend and somebody forgot to turn it back on this morning.

- The microphone makes a high-pitched noise.
- The screen is too small for the position of the projector.
- They are repainting the stripes in the parking lot so half of it is closed.
- The phone in the back of the room is ringing off the hook.

Well, you get the idea. And this is not fiction. All of the above have happened to me. Those kind of things will unnerve anybody. They drive me to panicsville.

You can avoid these kind of problems by doing a good job of planning and communicating with the host, coordinator, leader, or whoever is in charge. Leave nothing to chance. Review your requirements in advance and in detail. The last thing you want or need is a surprise.

The following is a combination checklist for planning and a "To Do" list when you arrive. The single most important item is, "Whom to call for help." You need the name, availability, and number of someone who has the authority and the wherewithal to fix things on short notice. In fact, I would recommend that you have that person meet you in the room when you arrive one hour early. If there isn't something that needs fixing or changing, it will be a miracle.

Facilities

_____	Who to call for help and the phone number (Home and office)
_____	Restroom location
_____	Phone location
_____	Snacks location
_____	Stairs/elevators location
_____	Fire alarm procedures
_____	Signs for directions to meeting
_____	Parking accommodations
_____	Location of copy machine

Room

_____ Check light controls and set level

_____ Temperature controls

_____ Disconnect phone in your room

_____ Smokers' section

_____ Ashtrays (smokers section only)

_____ Chairs/tables—number and arrangement

_____ Extension cord

_____ Pencil sharpener

_____ Electrical cords taped down

_____ Coat rack

_____ Lectern

_____ Water pitcher and glasses

_____ Clock

_____ Location of electrical outlets

_____ Adapter plug—three-prong to two-prong

_____ Position of spot lights

Overhead Projector

_____ Spare bulb

_____ Focused

_____ Cleaned of fingerprints and lint

_____ First transparency in place

Slide Projector

_____ Spare bulb

_____ Focused

_____ Tray cued to slot one

_____ Opaque slide in hole one

Movie Projector

_____ Check bulb

_____ Focused and set to fill screen

_____ Sound level check

_____ Film cued up to title frame

Music

_____ Cued

_____ Sound level check

Screen

_____ Location

_____ Size

Flip Chart

_____ Paper supply

_____ Magic Markers

_____ Check for dry ink in markers

_____ Rubber band across top

Microphone

_____ Lavaliere attachment

_____ Extra cord length for movement

_____ Sound check

_____ Back-up mike

Board

_____ Chalk

_____ Eraser

_____ Clean

Refreshments

_____ Coffee

_____ Decaffeinated

_____ Tea

_____ Juice

_____ Soft drinks

_____ Other

Audience Supplies

_____ Note pads

_____ Pencils

_____ Handouts

_____ Place cards

_____ Badges

_____ Roster

_____ Agenda

Final MiniRehearsal

_____ Opening

_____ Sequence check

_____ Close

Let's get back to those sweaty palms. The nervousness and anxiety peaks just before the presentation and during the first two or three minutes. You will hear presenters say, "If I can just make it through the first two minutes I'll be alright."

There are three things we can do in advance to reduce the anxiety and heighten our confidence.

The first thing we can do to get those butterflies in formation is the last item on our checklist. It's the final minirehearsal. I know you've already rehearsed. But as the coach says, "Let's do it one more time"—not in total, just three key items.

We have a solution to the anxiety of the first two minutes. The solution is to memorize the opening. If we have done this, the butterflies don't matter. We just open our mouths and out it comes. We don't even have to think about it. The simple logic is that by the time the opening is over, the butterflies are also over. Works like a charm. So we want one final rehearsal of the opening. Stand up in front and do and say the opening just as you have planned it. That way it will be super-fresh on your mind. Just that knowledge will improve your confidence.

Next we want to quickly flip through the body of the presentation. This is a final review of the material, and also a final check for the correct sequence. Also try a few of the visual aids. This will give you a final check of the equipment, the focus, the proper lighting, the centering on the screen, and so on.

Finally, rehearse the close. Remember that the close is the most important part of the presentation. Accordingly, we have memorized the close. Let's say it one more time and make it superfresh in our minds.

Now we are ready for the second thing we can do to control the butterflies. We want to greet, meet, and talk with some of the early arrivals. Where are they from? What do they do? This has an amazing effect. When you stand up in front, they are not an audience. They are warm, friendly people, several of whom you've just met. They are not the enemy. They are people just like you who are here because they want to be here, and want to hear what you have to say. The ones you've met, you liked, and they seemed to have liked you. So from the moment you stand up you are already among friends. But only if you've met and talked with them before the program starts. Don't go off by yourself. If you do, the only thing you will think about are weak knees, a squeaky voice, and shaky hands. And the more you think about it, the worse it will get. Just the opposite happens when you force yourself to meet and talk with the people. You get your mind off yourself, and on to the people. As a by-product you will pick up tidbits you can relate to or reference in your presentation.

The other side of this coin is that the people are interested in you. They expect you to be an expert on the subject you are going to talk about, but they also want you to be a regular guy or gal in other ways. They do not want you to be aloof, or distant, or an authority figure. They want to know that you are a warm, friendly person. That you are one of them. Don't disappoint them. "Reach out and touch someone." Try shaking hands with the folks on the front row.

The more you know about the audience, and the more they know about you, the more at ease you all will feel. You will not be strangers, but people who have come together for a slice of time to share a common interest.

The third thing you can do is release some tension. Here's how we do this. If you're sitting in a chair waiting to be introduced, reach down on both sides and grab the bottom of the seat. Pull up hard for five seconds. Release, then repeat several times. What you are doing is releasing tension. If you have a table in front of you, you can extend both arms under the table, palms up, and press up for five seconds. If you don't have a chair or a table, you can get the same results by pressing palm against palm.

Finally, take some deep breaths. If your heart's beating fast and you're taking short breaths, then you are using only the top one-third of your lungs. Poison is collecting in the bottom two-thirds. So take some deep breaths. Get that poison out.

And if all else fails, you can partake of the miracle drug of the decade. The miracle drug of the decade for presenters is physical fitness. Preparation and rehearsal are the only things better than physical fitness for controlling nerves and anxiety.

So if you've been on the fence and need another straw to persuade you to make the decision to shape up, here it is. For some people it may be more than a straw—it may be a sledge hammer. I've noticed that one of the more common characteristics of professional motivational speakers is their interest in physical fitness. They use it to control their bodies and recover from jet lag. The voice of experience says that if you jog three miles the morning of your presentation, you will have no problem with the jitters.

Do not—I repeat, *do not*—take man-made, mind-changing drugs for your nerves. They create a deceptive illusion. You will think you are doing better, but you will be doing worse. And worse than worse, you may find yourself on a one-way street.

In summary, if you keep your mind occupied with other people and positive thoughts, there will be no room for sweaty palms.

- You know 10 to 20 times more about the subject than anyone in the room.
- They are here because they want to be here.
- They like you and want you to succeed.
- You are well-prepared.
- Your presentation is well-organized and thoughtfully constructed.
- You have memorized a well-thought-out opening.
- Your visual aids are well-designed and will enhance your presentation.
- You have a solid case and a strong close.
- The audience is open-minded and receptive to new ideas.

Sometimes I just can't wait to get going. And if at any time I feel a little nervous, I will just look out at the audience and imagine that they are all sitting there stark naked. That will surely get your mind off your nerves.

CHAPTER 17

Getting Good, Getting Better—The Critique

Is the applause at the end a recognition of a good presentation, or a celebration that it's finally over?

If you have followed the Blueprint for Success and rehearsed, then you cannot fail. But you can get better. However good you are today, you can be two times better tomorrow. We get better by doing two things:

- Rehearsing and doing
- Fixing the flaws

We have covered the subject of rehearsing, so let's focus on fixing the flaws.

Like the game of golf, practice will make you better—up to a point. If, however, there is a fundamental flaw in what you are doing, no amount of practice will correct it. To correct it, the flaw must first be identified, and then corrective action taken.

In presenting as in golf, you will probably be the last to know what your flaws are. The good news is that once you find out what your weaknesses are, they are easier to correct than your golf game.

You can identify and correct the problems in your presentation by the use of technology, or the use of human beings. For best results, we recommend both.

The most powerful tool for identifying flaws is the videotape. It is also good for correcting the obvious. The impact of seeing yourself do the same stupid thing over and over is like being hit with a cold bucket of water. You will grit your teeth and swear that you will never do that again. In the world of presenting there is nothing that will give you religion as fast as seeing yourself sinning on camera. Interesting that the video camera is also used to identify the sins of the golf swing.

If you don't have access to video, you can at least borrow a cassette recorder and tape the audio portion of your presentation. This will allow you to easily identify problems in the area of pitch, pace, volume, pauses, and so forth.

The video and cassette tape also give you a record of questions asked by the audience. You need to carefully think through the questions. Consistent questions are a clue that your explanation is incomplete or confusing. They may also indicate areas of interest to the audience that had not occurred to you.

The videotape and audio cassette are strong medicine for correcting the obvious. But in some ways, we are our own worst critics. It has to do with ego and authorship—very human traits. Thus, video is not enough. Like the golfer trying to improve, you need professional help. Get it from an independent, unbiased, but critical observer whose judgment you respect, and who will give you candid comments.

The best observer or critic is someone who is experienced in giving presentations themselves. It might be an associate, a colleague, a member of a professional group, or someone who is on the program with you. If nothing else, pick a friend whose judgment you respect. In fact, it will be helpful if you can arrange for multiple people to critique your presentation.

What you want them to do is *not* give you the big picture, where we ask them at the end of our presentation the question, "Well, what did you think of it?" What you want is a detailed evaluation of the components of your presentation under the major critical categories of organization, preparedness, presentation skills, visual aids, and appearance. To accomplish this, we need to place in the hands of our critics a detailed checklist of items to evaluate.

Remember that we are looking for flaws: very specific areas that need improvement. While the critics are at it, we would like to also know our major strengths. This will keep us out of a deep depression when we review our flaws. So we need a checklist that is designed to identify our major strengths and our major weaknesses.

Brace yourself. This is going to hurt. Avoid the temptation to become defensive and start explaining the reasons why you do or don't do certain things. The audience doesn't know or care why you do or don't. The simple rule of this game is: The audience is right and you are wrong. So listen to your critics.

The following is an example of an evaluation form for use by your critics.

It's also helpful to get structured feedback directly from the audience. Audience critiques must of necessity be more general than the detailed critique checklist we have just reviewed. But general audi-

GETTING GOOD, GETTING BETTER

E= Excellent	S = Satisfactory	N = Needs Improvement
EXCELLENT ORGANIZATION	CIRCLE ONE E, S, N	NEEDS IMPROVEMENT
Clear statement of objective	E, S, N	Not sure what objective was
Well thought-out and rehearsed opening	E, S, N	Slow shaky start, not well rehearsed
Good structure and logical flow	E, S, N	Disjointed - does not flow well
Used hot spice to get attention and keep interest	E, S, N	Lost attention and interest of audience
Good summary, with strong close	E, S, N	Did not summarize, inconclusive finish
Good distribution of time	E, S, N	Too much time on some things, too little on others
Began on time, finished on time	E, S, N	Began late, ran overtime

FIGURE 17A Getting Good, Getting Better.

EXCELLENT	E, S, N	NEEDS IMPROVEMENT
PREPAREDNESS		
Well prepared, well rehearsed, knows material	E, S, N	Not well prepared, not well rehearsed, not sure of material
PRESENTATION SKILLS		
Friendly, relaxed, confident	E, S, N	Nervous, defensive
Enthusiastic, inspiring	E, S, N	Dull, dry, and boring
Humor appropriate for personality	E, S, N	Not natural, ineffective, poor taste
Good questions and audience participation	E, S, N	No questions, little or no audience participation
Used good examples and analogies	E, S, N	Poor examples, few analogies
Strong audible voice with variations	E, S, N	Weak monotone voice
Precise and natural words appropriate for the audience	E, S, N	Over use of slang, jargon and acronyms without definition
Good eye contact	E, S, N	Stares at floor, ceiling, space or screen

FIGURE 17A continued

EXCELLENT	E, S, N	NEEDS IMPROVEMENT
Natural stage movement	E, S, N	Frozen in one spot or racehorse
Varied pace	E, S, N	Consistently too fast or too slow
Smooth, strong gestures	E, S, N	Few gestures or jerky and unnatural
No bad habits or distracting mannerisms	E, S, N	You have the following bad habits and mannerisms_____ _____ _____
VISUAL AIDS		
Neat and easy to read	E, S, N	Sloppy and hard to read
Correct spelling and grammar	E, S, N	Misspellings, meaning not clear
Color enhanced	E, S, N	Too many colors, distracting
Used to clarify, simplify and emphasize	E, S, N	Too many, too wordy, too busy
Used multiple visual aid devices	E, S, N	Used only one visual aid device

FIGURE 17A continued

EXCELLENT	E, S, N	NEEDS IMPROVEMENT
Good use of pictures diagrams, graphs, bar charts, pie charts, etc.	E, S, N	Words and numbers only
Focused, centered and operated well	E, S, N	Did not check out in advance
APPEARANCE		
Professional appearance	E, S, N	Inappropriate attire
Comfortable, relaxed posture	E, S, N	Stiff or slouched
Body language accented and complemented presentation	E, S, N	Body language in conflict with words

FIGURE 17A continued

ence critiques, when used in conjunction with the detailed checklist, will allow you to really zero in and fine tune your presentation.

The difficulty with audience critiques is that they tend to be too general. If a critique sheet says the presentation was poor and of little value, that doesn't tell you a lot about what to do to correct it.

And don't fall into the 90 percent trap. People who run seminars and classes like the general critiques with five boxes to check.

- Excellent
- Very good
- Good
- Little value
- Poor

The wording of the questions are such that when summarized you can often make the statement, "Ninety percent of the attendees rated the seminar or the class as either excellent or very good."

That 90 percent sounds good, but here's the problem. Let's suppose it was a seminar on a small business computer for CPAs. The following day your competitor also had a seminar for CPAs. Unknown to you, 98 percent of the attendees rated the competitor's seminar as "excellent" or "very good."

The bottom line is that you thought you ran an excellent seminar, but the prospects decided to do business with someone else.

It's possible to design and word an audience critique to give you better information about acceptance or agreement, in addition to information about the presentation itself. Let's not forget our objective.

Figure 17B is an example of an audience critique.

In our quest for getting good and getting better, it's also helpful to observe other good presentations—especially presentations on the same subject. Take along a copy of the checklist. If you check off the list item by item, I think you will find that good presenters do well what we have now learned how to do.

All this criticizing will result in a list of a few areas that need improvement. What we must do now is prioritize the list. It is not possible to work on all areas at the same time. So pick the big one that stands out the most and work on it first. Then you can move on to the other areas.

Audience critiques can be a humbling experience. Remember we said that out of every 100 people there's at least one nut. They will sure show themselves on the critiques. You won't meet everyone's expectations. Some will be bored—a few may be hostile. So don't be surprised and don't take it personally. Even the President of the United States gets some bad reviews.

There was a fellow a long time ago who got terrible critiques. An example of one of his critiques is Figure 17C. They were so bad that it's hard to believe that he was so good. But he was. In fact, he is known today as one of the greatest teachers in all of recorded history. Maybe you've heard of him.

	Excel-lent	Very Good	Good	Little Value	Bad
Overall—What did you think of the presentation?					
I thought the content was					
I thought the presentation style was					
I thought the visual aids were					

	Yes	Maybe	No
Do you agree with the recommended plan?			
Do you plan to use it?			

I wish you had spent less time on:

_____

_____

_____

I wish you had spent more time on:

_____

_____

_____

I wish you had also discussed: _____

_____

_____

Other remarks and suggestions: _____

_____

_____

FIGURE 17B Example of an audience critique.

CRITIQUE

E = Excellent   S = Satisfactory   N = Needs Improvement

CATEGORY	RATING	REMARKS
Objective	E, S,(N)	Not sure what objective was
Structure & Flow	E, S,(N)	No planned structure
Preparedness	E, S,(N)	No signs of advanced preparation
Participation	E, S,(N)	Over-use of questions
Bad Habits	E, S,(N)	Interrogates person asking questions
Visual Aids	E, S,(N)	No visual aids
Confidence	E, S,(N)	Not sure of himself, always asking questions
Time Control	E, S,(N)	Never finishes at a scheduled time
Control	E, S,(N)	Too flexible, loses control
Close	E, S,(N)	Lets audience come to its own conclusions
Use of English	E, S,(N)	Speaks in heavy Greek accent
Appearance	E, S,(N)	Dresses in old sheet
Personality	E, S,(N)	Prone to suicide by poison

FIGURE 17C If your critiques aren't good—take heart. This fellow's weren't, either. His name was Socrates.

CHAPTER 18

The Road to Glory

All of us travel many roads. Some are crooked, some are bumpy, some lead us to a dead-end. But occasionally, either by plan or by accident, we find a smooth road that leads straight ahead to personal glory. Perhaps some of you are on such a road today. If you are, then the contents of this book can make your journey faster, smoother—and the glory greater.

If you have not yet found your road to glory, this may be your horse to ride. There is a critical shortage of good presenters. Whatever your profession or occupation, opportunity is knocking and inviting you into the spotlight.

Only a very few are willing to invest the time and effort to excel. For most the vision is blurred. They cannot see the road ahead. But if you have read this far, then you have a sense of personal destiny.

Good communicators can touch and change the lives of people. They can redirect the future of companies. You can be one of them. You have nothing to lose. You can only be better for the experience. So come along with me. Let's walk this road together. And I believe, *I believe*—I BELIEVE you will walk the road to glory.

INDEX

233